Neoliberalism

Key Concepts Series

Neoliberalism

Damien Cahill
Martijn Konings

Polity

First published in 2017 by Polity Press

Polity Press
65 Bridge Street
Cambridge CB2 1UR, UK

Polity Press
101 Station Landing
Suite 300
Medford, MA 02155
USA

ISBN-13: 978-0-7456-9552-5
ISBN-13: 978-0-7456-9553-2(pb)

A catalogue record for this book is available from the British Library.

Typeset in 10.5 on 12 pt Sabon
by Toppan Best-set Premedia Limited
Printed and bound in the UK by CPI Group Ltd, Croydon, CR0 4YY

The publisher has used its best endeavours to ensure that the URLs for external websites referred to in this book are correct and active at the time of going to press. However, the publisher has no responsibility for the websites and can make no guarantee that a site will remain live or that the content is or will remain appropriate.

Every effort has been made to trace all copyright holders, but if any have been inadvertently overlooked the publisher will be pleased to include any necessary credits in any subsequent reprint or edition.

For further information on Polity, visit our website:
politybooks.com

Contents

Acknowledgements

In writing this book, we have benefited from the help and insights of Melinda Cooper and David Primrose, as well as our colleagues in the Department of Political Economy, a collective of critically minded scholars of which we are proud to be part. Although this study does not deal with neoliberalism in the university, the managerial animosity that the mere existence of the department has provoked since we both joined about a decade ago stands as a constant reminder of the relevance of neoliberalism. Many thanks to Colin Crouch and one other anonymous referee, who offered very helpful comments on the manuscript. Louise Knight and Nekane Tanaka Galdos expertly guided the book to publication, offering both patience and encouragement when needed. Tim Clark did a wonderful job copy-editing the manuscript. Martijn Konings gratefully acknowledges research support from the Australian Research Council under grant number DE120100213. We would each like to thank our families for their love, patience and support.

Introduction

The death of former British Prime Minister Margaret Thatcher on 8 April 2013 met with deeply divided reactions, in Britain and elsewhere. She was honoured by the government of the day with a ceremonial funeral. *The Economist* (2013) celebrated her achievements, calling her a 'freedom fighter' and writing that 'what the world needs now is more Thatcherism, not less'. Many others, by contrast, had less fond memories of the period of Thatcher's prime-ministership: they recalled it above all as an organized assault upon their livelihoods and most cherished values, and they responded to the news of her death rather differently. For example, as Sky News reported, in the South Yorkshire town of Goldthorpe, 'many people had travelled from what remains of surrounding coal-fields to demonstrate that Baroness Thatcher's passing does not erase what they see as the hurt she inflicted on their lives and communities'. Attending a mock funeral, they sang 'Ding-dong! The witch is dead.'

The intense feelings and strong opinions provoked by Thatcher's death are testimony to the continued relevance of the political programme that she did so much to advance. As Prime Minister of Britain from 1979 to 1990, Margaret Thatcher was one of the most prominent advocates of what is now often called 'neoliberalism'. Through widespread privatization of state-owned enterprises, industry deregulation and a direct confrontation with powerful trade unions, she presided over a radical transformation of the British state and economy. During the following decades similar policies were implemented across the world, by parties of both right and left. This neoliberal policy revolution dismantled the key pillars of the postwar economic order that had been built amid the capitalist boom of the 1950s and 1960s, offering itself as a solution to problems such as inflation and economic stagnation that had emerged during the 1970s. The goal of this book is to understand and decode the widely debated and contested concept of neoliberalism.

While the era of Thatcher's prime-ministership ended in 1990, the effects of her policies were still being felt at the time of her death in 2013. The former mining communities who marked Thatcher's death with celebrations were still living with the devastating social and economic repercussions of the 1984–5 miners' strike, a bitter and violent year-long confrontation between the National Union of Miners and the Thatcher government that ended with the defeat of the union, led to the decimation of the mining industry and set the stage for the privatization of what remained. Moreover, while radical at the time, many of Thatcher's policies subsequently became political orthodoxy. Even the Labour Party, once fiercely opposed to 'Thatcherism', adopted many of its policies and implemented them while in office from 1997 to 2010. As *The Economist* (2013) argued, '[Labour Prime Minister] Tony Blair won several elections by offering Thatcherism without the rough edges.' Even today many would argue that the austerity policies pursued by governments around the world essentially represent a continuation of the sorts of policies pioneered by Thatcher.

One common way of understanding the neoliberal era is as embodying the rise of 'free markets'. Upon Thatcher's death, numerous media outlets reproduced this understanding, with statements such as 'Thatcher was master of the free market' (Hjelmgaard 2013) and references to her as 'a global champion of the late 20th-century free market revival' (White 2013). According to this view, politicians such as Thatcher in Britain, Ronald Reagan in the US, and many others subsequently, reduced the size of the state and the role of government within the economy, thus allowing for the flourishing of free markets unrestrained by public regulation.

Certainly the rhetoric of neoliberal politicians like Thatcher and Reagan consistently praised the virtues of free markets and railed against the stifling effects of big government and a bloated welfare state. Yet, the reality was often quite different. Under both Thatcher and Reagan state expenditure was not retrenched and, indeed, in Britain, the US and across much of the world, the neoliberal era gave birth to a whole host of new state regulations and regulatory institutions – widespread privatization and deregulation notwithstanding. As Vogel (1998) argues, it may well have resulted in a situation of 'freer markets', but it was simultaneously also one of 'more rules', as deregulation in practice involved significant economic and social re-regulation. Moreover, state activism did not by any means diminish. The Thatcher government, for example, deployed a militarized police force as well as the secret security services against the National Union of Miners. Meanwhile, the left-wing-dominated Greater London Council was abolished by the Thatcher government, and local councils more generally were denuded of many of their powers. These became increasingly centralized at the level of the national government. Such features led Andrew Gamble (1988) to describe Thatcherism as an ideology committed to both 'the free economy and the strong state'.

Neoliberalism transformed states across the world in ways that made people more dependent upon market mechanisms for accessing a range of social services. But an emphasis upon 'free' markets has often led commentators to miss the constituent features of such markets – not just the pervasive regulatory framework underpinning them, but also the agents who comprise markets, especially large corporations. Similarly, the tendency to view the neoliberal transformation of states as 'market-led' can obscure not only how such restructuring has created new avenues for large corporations to reshape public policy, but also the ways in which states have been reshaped to more closely resemble and operate like corporations (see Crouch 2011; Birch 2015; Wilkes 2013). Understanding neoliberalism therefore requires that we identify the reconfigured institutional relationships brought about through processes such as privatization, deregulation and new approaches to macroeconomic policy, and that we untangle and assess the various claims made about such processes.

Neoliberalism: a useful concept?

Margaret Thatcher was an admirer of Friedrich Hayek, who has since become recognized as one of the leading neoliberal intellectuals. After she was elected Prime Minister in 1979, Hayek wrote to congratulate her; Thatcher replied: 'I am very proud to have learnt so much from you over the past few years. I hope that some of those ideas will be put into practice by my Government in the next few months. As one of your keenest supporters I am determined that we should succeed. If we do, your contribution to our ultimate victory will have been immense' (quoted in Ebenstein 2001: 295). But although Thatcher had never made a secret of her admiration for Hayek, it is only over the past decade-and-a-half or so that scholars have begun to explore in greater depth the intellectual sources and ideological roots of the neoliberal project and of the policies and models it has sought to implement. Such contributions have tended to focus on the emergence of a distinctly neoliberal critique of 'collectivism' (especially as expressed in the postwar welfare state and the state-planned economies that existed in countries like Russia until the end of the 1980s) during the interwar period, the way this was elaborated through various strands of thinking in the following decades, and the ways in which it came over time to have a crucial influence on political transformations. In describing the transition from the postwar order to the neoliberal era these analyses have also tended to place a great deal of emphasis on the intentions, ideas and interests of elite actors as well as their ability to purposefully coordinate their actions and implement their political strategies. Examples of such approaches include well-known books – written by authors who otherwise differ significantly in theoretical and political commitments – such as David Harvey's *A Brief History of Neoliberalism* (2005), Naomi Klein's *The Shock Doctrine* (2008) and Philip Mirowski's *Never Let a Serious Crisis Go to Waste* (2013).

To a significant extent, it has been this wave of scholarship that has propelled the concept of neoliberalism to its current status as a key concept for understanding the contours of modern life. Until the early years of the twenty-first century, neoliberalism was perhaps more a 'word' than a 'concept' – that is, just a term used to refer to the general shift from the social-democratic and progressive-liberal era to policies and institutions that were more concerned to promote market mechanisms and were more friendly to business and capital. As such, the word was used mostly as an adjective in major debates focusing on related but different questions (such as globalization, industrial restructuring, and deregulation). The word certainly had a somewhat critical connotation and was unlikely to be used by those (e.g., many orthodox economists) who would typically view economic processes as being primarily about neutral measures of efficiency and growth (Boas and Gans-Morse 2009). Otherwise, however, the term itself did not appear to be particularly contentious and was certainly not the focal point of scholarly competition to define the character of contemporary capitalism.

More recent arguments, in contrast, have claimed that neoliberalism is much more than just a useful descriptor – that it is in fact a discrete project whose origins can be traced back to the interwar period and which came into its own during the 1970s, when powerful organizations and political forces gravitated around the neoliberal intellectual tradition and gave it financial backing and institutional materiality. Subsequently, this forced perspectives that until then had used the word in a more casual way to make explicit how they view the neoliberal phenomenon. Although there is no shortage of rival definitions of neoliberalism, and many have been willing to associate themselves with one definition or another, a pronounced trend has been to insist that the concept should not or cannot be neatly defined. In the course of these debates, the growing interest in neoliberalism as a discrete political project, with distinctive ideational antecedents, has been matched by a growing scepticism regarding the use of the term. It is seen, in Mudge's words, as 'an oft-invoked but ill-defined concept' (2008: 703). One often hears that it is a somewhat lazy way for left-wing critics to group together any number of heterogeneous things to which they happen to be opposed. Imprecision would seem to characterize its use, sometimes even among those for whom the concept is central to their analysis, and its over-use is seen to have resulted in a loss of analytical value. This has led some to argue that scholars would be best served by jettisoning it as an unhelpful label, or, at the very least, by specifying the concept as being applicable only to a greatly narrowed range of phenomena. Venugopal, for example, argues that 'much of what is explained – and hence left under-explained – as neoliberal can benefit, if it were simply to be disconnected from this universalizing framework and if neoliberalism were to be reconceptualised down in a sharper and unambiguous way to one of its constituent forms' (2015: 181). Others point to what they view as a disconnect between neoliberal theory and the major transformations to states and economies effected through processes of deregulation and privatization (Braithwaite 2008).

But, of course, the notion of a strict correspondence of concept and reality rarely provides a good basis from which to evaluate the usefulness of concepts. By their nature, the labels we use represent abstractions, approximations and ideal types. Social-science scholarship tends to characterize political economic regimes, modes of regulation and forms of state with reference to the normative doctrines to which their supporters profess allegiance: Keynesianism, socialism, liberalism, etc. A label such as neoliberalism is of course not by itself capable of capturing the messy, complex dynamics and variegated details of social formations. The question is rather whether it provides a useful entry point, a way of looking at these processes that can subsequently be enriched with empirical detail. The phenomena of human life are inherently more complex than the social-scientific concepts we use to comprehend them, but this truism should not be used to fudge the issue of the relevance of neoliberalism. The labels we use are in many respects less important than our description of the political economic processes to which the label refers. In the next section we will survey some of the main approaches to neoliberalism in order to lay the groundwork for presenting our own perspective.

Perspectives on neoliberalism

It is useful to start here with what we might call the 'classic' perspective on neoliberalism, which saw it in terms of the growing power of markets vis-à-vis the institutions of national states. We find here a very literal interpretation of the 'neo' in 'neoliberalism': it is seen as a revival of or return to classic laissez-faire liberalism, marked domestically by a return to the minimal state and internationally by the resubordination of national policy priorities to the forces of economic and financial globalization (see, e.g., Przeworski 1992; Boyer and Drache 1996; Stiglitz 2002). For many purposes, this is a useful way of thinking about the changes neoliberalism has set in motion. But the tendency of thinkers in this vein to quickly qualify their basic assertions about the decline of the state suggests that the model has clear limitations. That is to say, it often has major difficulty accounting for those aspects of neoliberalism that do not fit with the idea of a return to a laissez-faire state.

This economic focus can be contrasted to the tendency to put neoliberal ideas and theories at the centre of analysis – a tendency that has been pronounced in recent contributions. Many ideational accounts emphasize how neoliberal ideas have developed historically and the organizational forms through which this has occurred. Typically this entails a close reading of the texts produced by key neoliberal intellectuals, the ways in which these have been translated by neoliberal think tanks, and the relationships forged between the latter and political and economic elites. For some scholars, such analysis is primarily an exercise in intellectual history that seeks to understand the diversity of currents that comprise the neoliberal intellectual movement and the sometimes nuanced differences between its leading figures (e.g., Nik-Khah 2011; Burgin 2012; Ebenstein 2015). But it is increasingly common for such scholars either to treat neoliberal ideas as the key to deciphering the logic of the neoliberal policy revolution or to see a fairly straight causal line from the formulation of neoliberal ideas to the implementation of neoliberal policy models, uncovering the hidden machinations of neoliberal think tanks and their attempts to shift the prevailing climate of opinion.

Emblematic of the latter tendency is Naomi Klein's widely read *The Shock Doctrine* (which, while written by a journalist for a popular audience, has also had a major scholarly impact). For Klein, political elites in the thrall of Milton Friedman and others from the Chicago School of economics, and in particular Friedman's statement that 'Only a crisis – actual or perceived – produces real change' (quoted in Klein 2008: 7), would be key to the advance of neoliberalism. According to Klein, neoliberalism was constructed through the ways these elites managed to seize opportunistically on natural disasters, war and economic crises to force the dystopian neoliberal free market ideal on disoriented populations. More recently, Mirowski (2013) has put forward a thesis of ideational causation to explain the rise of neoliberalism. His focus is on the 'neoliberal thought collective' represented by the network of think tanks centred on the Mont Pelerin Society, which mobilized from the 1940s onwards to shift elite opinion in a neoliberal direction. He recognizes that neoliberalism entails neither a weakened or smaller state nor free markets. Rather, he argues that the neoliberal thought collective, as well as intellectuals such as Hayek and Friedman, deliberately sought to cultivate an image of neoliberalism as concerned with the freeing of markets by limiting the state, all the while recognizing that any form of state action, including authoritarianism, was consistent with constructing a competitive economic order based on private property.

For Mirowski, then, neoliberalism is a 'Schmittian' project: a form of government that works by paralysing or bypassing the normal rules of democracy. Carl Schmitt was a German political and legal theorist associated with the Nazi regime. He criticized liberal democracy for the ways it covered up the antagonism that he considered foundational to politics. For Schmitt, it was naively idealistic to think that authority could ever be fully consensual or rationally grounded in coherent norms arrived at through collective decision making. Authority in the end was always 'exceptional': not derived from democratic norms but rooted in the force of decision. Many critical intellectuals have found in Schmitt's thought a useful model of how neoliberalism works in practice, namely by sidelining or even suspending democratic institutions. In public, Mirowski argues, the neoliberal thought collective advocated free markets and small states, but in their own private discussions and meetings with policy elites they advocated the enforcement of market rule by states. He describes this as 'the double truth doctrine' – a strategy whereby 'an elite would be tutored to understand the deliciously Schmittian necessity of repressing democracy, while the masses would be regaled with ripping tales of "rolling back the nanny state" and being set "free to choose" – by convening a closed Leninist organization of counter-intellectuals' (Mirowski 2013: 86).

If we take Mirowski's account as the limit point of the idealist take on neoliberalism, it readily bears out some of its shortcomings. Its tendency to reduce the neoliberal transformation of states to far-sighted manipulation on the part of a small group of intellectuals is unconvincing. Certainly conspiracies exist, and we may readily grant that the Mont Pelerin Society is as close to one as we may ever hope to find evidence of, but the mere discovery of a conspiracy should not lead us to assume that it must have succeeded in realizing its goals in the way it intended. In other words, we should not assume that neoliberalism can *only* rise to power through bypassing democratic institutions and the popular will. As a blanket statement this is untenable, even if neoliberalism has involved its fair share of vanguardist initiatives. Among the most telling examples here, what should we make of the many working-class British who voted for Thatcher, and the many working-class Americans who voted for Reagan? To say that these people were simply misled by the 'double truth' machinations of neoliberal elites is to revert to a crude notion of ideology that has been widely discredited, and for good reason.

Of course not all arguments made in this vein are as uncompromising as Mirowski's. But there is nonetheless a pronounced tendency to view the neoliberal project as characterized by a deep affinity with exceptionalism and authoritarianism (e.g., Bruff 2014; Streeck 2015; Bonefeld 2016). We should not, however, be too quick to brand neoliberalism an undemocratic doctrine that elites can only ever impose through bypassing democratic procedures. After all, avowedly neoliberal programmes have often enjoyed remarkable electoral support. Stuart Hall (1979) observed the popular traction of Thatcherism and proposed the idea of 'authoritarian populism' to capture the paradoxical dynamics at work. Seen from such an angle, the emphasis on neoliberalism's anti-democratic credentials appears rather one-sided, as it ignores the powerful ways in which neoliberal discourses have often been able to mobilize a great deal of popular support. This does not mean, however, that we should replace one blanket characterization with another. The point is precisely that we should be attuned to the differences in the ways neoliberalism has manifested itself in different regions and political systems. To say that neoliberalism often has an undemocratic streak – that it views the gains of democracy as having gone too far and as threatening the basic liberties of a market order – should not blind us to the obvious differences between its manifestations, such as those between the UK (where Thatcher came to power through an election) and Chile (where neoliberalism had to ally itself to military power in order to capture the state).

Still other scholars understand neoliberalism as the product of institutional variables. Such approaches tend to reject the idea that real-world transformations simply mirror the prescriptions of neoliberal theory, and they focus instead on empirically identifying the actual development of pro-market and pro-business policy shifts, investigating how nationally specific institutional architectures mediate the adoption and implementation of neoliberal ideas (Prasad 2006; Heyes, Lewis and Clark 2012). For example, Fourcade-Garinchas and Babb (2002) show how local institutional structures shaped the adoption of neoliberalism in four national contexts. They identify the emergence of an 'ideological' form of neoliberalism in Britain and Chile in contrast to a more 'pragmatic' version in France and Mexico, largely based on the degree to which each nation's domestic postwar institutional architecture promoted conflict or consensus. Such institutionalist approaches alert us to the unevenness, variegation and contextual specificity evident in the roll-out of neoliberalism globally. Moreover, by highlighting the fact that privatizations and deregulations often led in practice to a proliferation of new regulations, the rich empirical studies in this tradition of analysis also provide a useful corrective to the overly simplistic view of neoliberalism as a programme of rolling back the state.

But where this literature is less robust is in explaining what forces are at work, amid all the diversity of institutional dynamics and outcomes, such that the use of a generalizing concept like neoliberalism is required. Some authors working in this perspective have pursued this line of reasoning, arguing that there is no meaningful correspondence between the normative precepts of neoliberal theory on the one hand and the practices of contemporary restructuring on the other. Braithwaite, for example, thinks that we have little more than a 'neoliberal fairytale' (2008: 4). Along similar lines, aligning himself with perspectives that emphasize the importance of institutional varieties among different national systems, Block (2012) argues that we may as well dispense with the very concept of capitalism altogether (if we talk continuously about institutional variety, his reasoning goes, then at some point we need to stop assuming that these configurations are all different 'varieties of capitalism' and instead raise the question 'varieties of what?'). In other words, the institutionalist literature tends to be insufficiently concerned with the systemic dynamics of the capitalist economy and the common pressures it imposes (Albo 1996; Coates 2000). Even though the global economic crisis of the 1970s is often seen as a catalyst for the changes being analysed, in many institutional accounts the global economy remains in the background, forming the crucial context for the story of institutional transformation, yet not amenable to explanation by the conceptual tools of institutional analysis itself. In reducing the question of neoliberalism to a purely empirical one, it seems that we may be missing out on some of its key aspects as well as its distinctive significance.

Neoliberalism: a critical synthesis

Here we follow the lead of other scholars, such as Brenner, Peck and Theodore (2010), who share a concern to avoid overly idealist explanations and to incorporate institutional factors into their analysis, but remain throughout concerned to formulate a critique of neoliberalism as a distinctive political project (for approaches in a similar vein, see Jessop 2002; Wacquant 2012; Cahill 2014). There is more at stake in specifying this content than the need to 'combine' material and ideational factors in our account of neoliberalism. That is certainly part of it, but such formulations do not by themselves solve the problem. As Dardot and Laval (2013:

8) point out, some Marxist accounts of neoliberalism (e.g., Duménil and Lévy 2004) adopt such an approach in ways that reproduce the problems of each perspective, combining a materialist focus on economic structures with a strong emphasis on the role of ideology and specific political projects in the rise of neoliberalism. In such a perspective, neoliberal elites appear as simply facilitating the rebirth of capitalism, as the midwives of a process that otherwise follows its own autonomous logic. While such Marxist perspectives usefully situate the rise of neoliberalism within the class dynamics and contradictions inherent to capitalism, they do little to bring into view the distinctive character of neoliberalism and they continue to rely on a separation of economics from politics and ideology. That is, they are unable to provide a compelling account of the connections between politics and economics in the rise of neoliberalism.

Dardot and Laval (2013: 9) note that even though Harvey's (2005) prominent work is characterized by similar problems, it makes an important innovation by insisting that the (re)production of neoliberal economic structures is always dependent on the kind of political interventions that Harvey associates with the idea of the permanence of 'accumulation by dispossession' – which represents a reworking of Marx's concept of 'primitive accumulation' to capture the ways in which neoliberalism dispossesses ordinary people through state-led processes such as privatization. This idea is not without connections to the Schmittian theme of exceptionalism, but rather than embracing that idea in its most dramatic form to outline an idealist theory of neoliberalism, it suggests a more plausible way to think about the constitutive connections between economic structures and politics.

We can draw here on Wood's (1995) work, which rejects the notion that we can talk about politics and economics as if they were inherently different spheres of human activity. Instead, Wood argues, the separation of politics from economics is itself an institutional construction of a specifically capitalist character, a historical process through which the social relations of capitalism are created. Under feudalism power and class relations were directly political, more or less immediately backed up by force. Capitalism, by contrast, is based on principles of private property and legal equality:

exploitation and domination are now no longer overtly political but become 'hidden' in the economic domain, where they take on more indirect and mediated qualities. In other words, the separation of the political and the economic is not in the nature of things, but is ideological. And, as the dividing line is always contested, the history of capitalism is consequently characterized by the continuous resurgence of state power. To understand this as 'exceptionalist' is simply to set too much store by the official appearances and formal discourses of capitalist institutions: institutional interventions are the lifeblood of capitalism. Neoliberalism, then, is, as Panitch says of globalization, 'both...authored by states and...primarily about reorganising, rather than bypassing states' (1994: 63).

Neoliberalism is characterized by a certain degree of comfort with the constitutive character of institutional interventions: at its heart is an awareness that its success is not in fact predicated on the realization of some utopian state of non-intervention, whatever its official slogans might declare and however important promises to get the state out of people's business are for its political legitimacy. It is this focus on the institutional transformations effected by neoliberalism that can be usefully elaborated through an engagement with the history of neoliberal ideas. Peck (2010) draws on that history, but less in order to identify the origins of the neoliberal project than to reveal new sources of insight into the distinctive logic of neoliberalism. As the title of his book suggests, he is interested in figuring out the contours of 'neoliberal reason', as a distinctive way of approaching questions of human conduct and social organization. In recent years, theorists have relied on expressions such as 'neoliberal reason' or 'neoliberal rationality' to steer the analysis of neoliberalism away from an exaggerated concern with the actions of small circles of political and ideological elites (e.g., Dardot and Laval 2013; Brown 2015; Konings 2018). This is meant to express the idea that the power of neoliberalism involves not just the top-down imposition of a regime overtly biased in favour of corporate and financial interests but is also rooted in a broader field of beliefs, practices and institutions.

A great deal of current thinking about neoliberalism along such lines takes its cue from the lecture courses delivered by Michel Foucault during the 1970s. Foucault's extensive discussion came as something of a surprise when it appeared in English translation during the first decade of the twenty-first century, because until that time, in so far as Foucaultian scholarship was interested in contemporary transformations, it had focused primarily on evolving governmentalities and subjectivities and had sought to steer attention away from precisely the focus on epochal transformations or neoliberalism as a distinct political project (e.g., Rose 1993). But in the *Birth of Biopolitics* (2008 [1979]), Foucault engaged at length with the history of neoliberalism. Central to his argument was the notion that neoliberalism should not be reduced to a simple attempt to revive or return to classic liberalism, the set of doctrines that had enjoyed their heyday in nineteenth-century Britain and that instructed governments to desist from continuous interventions and instead adopt laissez-faire policies that would result in higher levels of economic welfare. Whereas classic liberalism had always made strong claims about the natural legitimacy or self-evident efficiency of the market, neoliberal concerns were driven by an awareness that such properties could not be assumed and that the continued viability of capitalism required more than a faith in the natural efficiency of markets. For Foucault, this 'constructivist' streak is at the core of neoliberalism's distinctive rationality. Whereas classic liberalism saw its task as removing institutional obstacles to the logic of the market, neoliberalism accepts that the kind of market order it envisages needs to be actively constructed, institutionally and politically.

This was not an abstract intellectual shift but one rooted in a recognition that liberalism by itself had failed and that it could only be rescued through a thorough rethinking. In other words, for Foucault, neoliberalism needs to be understood as an engagement with the limitations of classic liberalism that had become manifest during the social and economic instability of the early twentieth century. Neoliberal ideas were first formulated during the interwar period, when capitalism experienced a crisis whose intensity may be difficult to imagine for those who have come of age during the neoliberal era. Capitalism was going through an extraordinary contraction, and this was a major factor in precipitating the collapse of the international liberal world order and the turn to economic nationalism. Under these circumstances, capitalism had lost much of its legitimacy, and capitalist elites' fear of the power of labour movements and the danger of communism can hardly be overestimated. Rather than a doctrinaire reassertion of classic liberalism, neoliberalism in its origins was marked by a serious engagement with socialist ideas and the aspirations of the labour movement.

As Plehwe (2009: 10) reports, the term neoliberalism was used first in the 1920s by authors who were specifically minded to defend liberal principles against advancing socialist forces. Plehwe (2009: 11) also observes that interwar Vienna served as something of an intellectual training ground for the neoliberal movement: there, Ludwig von Mises and Friedrich Hayek entered into debates with proponents of socialist policies that would eventually take the form of the 'socialist calculation debate', which questioned whether socialist central planning was capable of allocating economic resources efficiently (see Hayek 1949). Both realized acutely that, if orthodox economics was correct and markets were to be conceived as little more than neutral transactional devices (as in classic economic liberalism), then the case for capitalism being superior to socialism was on shaky ground. Their defence of capitalism was less concerned with the ideal efficiency of markets than with emphasizing the practical limitations of human knowledge and the way this undermines socialist ambitions for the transparent shaping of the future in line with collectivist principles (Gane 2014). Similarly, Walter Lippmann – whose book *The Good Society* (1937) became the occasion for a colloquium that played a seminal role in the emergence of a neoliberal intellectual movement – was a prominent progressive reformer who felt that classic liberalism had run its course but who had also begun to doubt progressivism's capacity to right its wrongs through benevolent institutionalist engineering.

In short, neoliberal doctrine originated in the rethinking of capitalism's foundations in a context where classic liberalism could no longer readily claim the mantle of historical progress. As an intellectual project, neoliberal thought can be viewed as an attempt to reformulate the principles of classic liberalism at a time when the latter had lost much of its legitimacy. This involved a recognition that liberalism had its own problems and that a revitalization of capitalism could not simply involve a return to earlier times. In a sense, neoliberalism is rooted in an appreciation of what Karl Polanyi (1944) would later come to think of as the impossibility of the liberal utopia of endless market disembedding – the process whereby the economy becomes unhitched from its social moorings. This often eludes many contemporary critics of neoliberalism, who have converged en masse around Polanyi's work as a foundation for the critique of neoliberalism (Blyth 2002; Fraser 2014; Block and Somers 2014), all too often without realizing that neoliberals themselves had already grappled with very similar issues and proposed particular solutions to make capitalism viable again. That certainly does not mean that we need to retreat from the critique of neoliberalism, but it does mean that we should be careful not merely to accuse neoliberals of maintaining a naive belief in the virtues of the free market. Neoliberalism is more complicated – and more interesting – than such simplistic critiques would suggest.

This has important implications, which we will explore throughout this book. First, to acknowledge that neoliberalism involved a reflexive engagement with the limits of free markets, rather than simply being an attempt to restore the classic liberal dystopia, entails recognizing the ways in which the neoliberal project has been minded to produce its own legitimacy – it has at times succeeded in this and at other times failed, but it has never been uninterested in this question. This makes comprehensible, for instance, the role of 'ordoliberalism' in postwar Germany: one of the more interesting findings of recent work on the history of neoliberalism has been the extent to which the design of the German 'social market economy' of the early postwar era was influenced by neoliberal thinkers (Ptak 2009). In other words, the postwar state involved not just social-democratic politicians and labour movements pushing back against capitalism but also liberal thinkers practically implementing their understanding of the preconditions for a viable and sustainable capitalist order. This also means that, even as neoliberalism can credibly be described as a political revolution, we should remain alert to elements of continuity: many neoliberal policies worked only because of the ways in which the Keynesian era had managed to incorporate the population into a distinctly capitalist order, giving them a stake in its coherent operation.

Similar considerations allow us to make sense of the alliance between neoliberalism and neoconservatism. For many years this was understood as a mostly idiosyncratic and circumstantial affiliation, dependent on the ways foreign-policy hawks advanced the corporate agenda and the possibility of manipulating an electorate of religious 'value-voters' (Frank 2005). But events of recent years have shown that there is a deeper connection here: as phenomena like the populist Tea Party movement have demonstrated, neoliberal ideas can organically connect to sources of popular enthusiasm for the restoration of a fairer form of capitalism (Konings 2015). This means that, while it is fair to say that in important ways neoliberalism has limited the reach of democratic decision making by replacing it with economic criteria, we should not be too quick to view this as a 'depoliticization' of contemporary society. The task is rather to explain how neoliberalism has been produced and maintained through contending social and political forces.

Second, there are also implications for questions of imperialism and international power. If neoliberalism should be understood as responding to the limitations of classic liberalism, this includes an engagement with the sources of international breakdown during the interwar period. At various times during recent decades commentators have anticipated a retreat of Western nations into economic nationalism and protectionism, as during the interwar period. But this has failed to materialize, and even the force of the 2007–8 global financial crisis has not triggered a fragmentation of the international economic order. Highlighting the crucial importance of the state in the making and reproduction of neoliberalism, we emphasize the role of the US state in particular. Here we follow Panitch and Gindin (2012), who argue that neoliberalism involves a new form of imperialism, which no longer simply turns on the relation between core and periphery but also involves the penetration of US institutions into other Western polities. This process, they argue, has provided the world economy with patterns of interdependence that serve to prevent its disintegration in the face of the destabilizing dynamics of capitalism. It is of course often recognized that the US has both promoted and benefited from the globalization of markets, but this relationship is always seen as precarious and fragile, characterized by a lack of coherent institutional mechanisms for the production of domestic and international order – reflecting above all a decline of the more stable hegemonic order of the Keynesian era. In this book we question such accounts, emphasizing the enduring – if never smooth – connection between neoliberalism and the role of the US state.

Third, our understanding of neoliberalism involves an emphasis on the role of finance. Finance has of course received much attention from scholars and other commentators, and recent years have seen the emergence of a large body of literature on 'financialization'. Indeed, many would prefer the latter concept over that of neoliberalism as a way to capture the character of contemporary capitalism. But the financialization literature has tended to approach finance as a more or less superstructural phenomenon: the expansion of finance is typically understood as reflecting an unresolved crisis in the real economy, serving as a means to postpone the contradictions of capitalism. Such perspectives understate the ability of the growth of finance to transform the structures of capitalism. In neoliberalism, it is no longer just corporations that invest; ordinary people too must become entrepreneurs and make speculative investments. At the limit, they must invest in their own skills and capacities (that is, their 'human capital') and become 'entrepreneurs of the self' (see Foucault 2008: ch. 9). Time and again, neoliberal capitalism has challenged assumptions about objective limits and pushed the logic of capitalization into new areas of human life. This is not to say that neoliberal finance is not crisis-prone – it clearly is. But the instability generated by finance is not simply a sign of its irrationality but rather a corollary of the dynamism it generates – and we should recognize that neoliberalism has displayed a remarkable ability to bounce back from such crises.

This volume, then, is driven by the conviction that neoliberalism is a key concept for understanding the era we live in. We have made the case that neoliberalism should not be separated from a more general understanding of capitalism:

neoliberalism is 'the contemporary mode of existence of capitalism' (Ayers and Saad-Filho 2015: 603). At the same time, however, we should not understand neoliberalism as simply a return to a basic form of capitalism. Rather, it represents an attempt to reconstruct capitalism in a way that registers some of the limitations of classic liberalism. Unlike the latter, neoliberalism does not take the existence or reproduction of capitalism for granted. It is keenly aware that markets are not natural phenomena that simply emerge when institutional obstacles are removed. This constructivist impulse lies at the heart of neoliberal reason, and it is why neoliberalism involves much more than simple deregulation. Nevertheless, the notion that free markets are the most efficient and desirable basis of human organization, and the claim that states are inherently inefficient, remain central to the logic and appeal of neoliberalism. These two poles of market construction and market freedom coordinate neoliberal reason, a rather malleable set of political heuristics that, from the 1970s, came to shape processes of political and economic transformation that had been set in motion by the crisis of the postwar order. It provided political and economic elites with modes of seeing, formatting and interpreting that, while certainly ideological, were also broadly compatible with the imperative to restructure faltering capital accumulation. A variety of factors were central to this restructuring: a much greater engagement of corporations in the delivery of social services through policies of privatization and marketization; the extensive deregulation of industries, the most far-reaching of which was financial deregulation in all its forms, which enabled financial capital to play a much more dominant role within the global economy and indeed, people's everyday lives; new approaches to macroeconomic policy, beginning with the dismantling of the Bretton Woods system of exchange-rate controls and culminating in a focus on low inflation and tolerance of much higher levels of unemployment than previously; and a confrontation with the power of labour unions. This resulted in a new institutional architecture for managing capitalist social relations, at both domestic and global levels, even if there was, and is, a deep temporal and geographic unevenness to this process.

The structure of this book

Chapter 1 gives an overview of the historical development of neoliberalism. The chapter discusses the emergence of a distinctly neoliberal discourse during the interwar period and the ways in which during the post-Second World War period neoliberal intellectuals began to organize themselves through different forums. Neoliberal ideas, however, could only become influential in a particular set of circumstances: it was during the crisis of the postwar order and its system of embedded liberalism that they gained political traction and became influential in practical terms. This should not be taken to mean, however, that the rise of neoliberalism to political power came about as an organic evolution of circumstances. Although, as we have argued in this introduction, we should be careful not to discount neoliberalism's ability to connect to popular concerns and to produce its own distinctive form of common sense, it is equally important to appreciate that its ascendancy was also characterized by a vanguard political movement that acquired viability amid a particular set of structural pressures. Reagan in the US and Thatcher in the UK came to political power by staging what can be thought of as a democratic revolution, working within the framework of electoral democracy while insisting that the social and political gains the system had permitted during previous decades were at the root of the problems of the 1970s. They advanced a point of view that was highly counterintuitive when assessed by the rationality that had governed embedded liberalism – by their neoliberal logic, it was no longer the institutions of the postwar welfare state that were under threat and in need of protection; rather, it was those very institutions that were preventing the proper operation of the market economy. The chapter discusses how, following the policy turns initiated by Reagan and Thatcher, neoliberal discourses and policy models spread and were adopted in a variety of institutional contexts. The period from the late 1980s until the first years of the twenty-first century can be seen as the era when neoliberalism became hegemonic, embedded in everyday practices and the routine norms and processes of policymaking. The chapter also traces how this heyday of neoliberalism came undone, highlighting both the role of changing economic conditions and growing political resistance. But it questions whether this has automatically meant the decline of neoliberalism: it has survived many announcements of its decline, and an ability to thrive on failure and to 'fail forward' (Peck 2010: 6) seems to be part of its arsenal. Although this book exposes a range of contradictions in the edifice of neoliberalism, exactly when those contradictions will become fatal must remain an open question.

As we have argued in this introduction, finance occupies a central place in the making and logic of neoliberalism, and Chapter 2 explores the relation between finance and neoliberalism in detail. US President Nixon's policy turn at the start of the 1970s, which ended the convertibility of US dollars into gold, had broken open the institutional edifice of embedded liberalism. The result was the accelerated growth and globalization of financial markets, which put a great deal of pressure on countries to move away from the policies they had pursued in earlier years. But the response to the instability and uncertainty that ensued during the 1970s was not always overtly political, and often had a more technocratic character: the 'Volcker shock' (the rapid increase in interest rates by the US Federal Reserve under the chairmanship of Paul Volcker) at the end of the decade was a response to inflationary pressures that increasingly militated against the ability of the US to attract capital inflows. This policy turn was remarkably effective in conquering domestic inflation and fortifying the US's position at the centre of international finance. It also gave a dramatic boost to the unfolding international debt crisis, bringing indebted developing countries under the control of the International Monetary Fund (IMF) and the World Bank and making foreign currency debt into the 'lever' for structural adjustment. Domestically, the Volcker policy forced the Reagan administration to push back against union-led wage rises and to cut into welfare programmes even more aggressively than it had originally intended. It also triggered a great deal of financial innovation, which would become a major factor in supporting processes of financial expansion that interacted in specific ways with growing socioeconomic inequality and stagnating wages. Like other accounts of neoliberal finance, the chapter highlights the tendency of finance to generate crises but it also points to the recurrent tendency of neoliberal financial institutions to bounce back from such instability. The volatility engendered by neoliberal finance may well indicate some of its limitations, but it is important not to pre-judge the issue (as critics have tended to do) and to acknowledge that it is not *a priori* clear what kind of financial crises neoliberalism can or cannot survive.

One of the most dramatic effects of the policy shifts of the early 1980s was the acceleration of deindustrialization and the growth of unemployment. Full employment had been a key ingredient of the postwar class compromise and the Keynesian state. Fordist manufacturing in Western countries had become subject to deindustrialization trends from the late 1960s, and the effects of this were reinforced by the erosion of traditional family structures and the rise of social forces that pushed against the limitations of the postwar welfare state (the women's movement, the civil rights movement in the US, but also the students' movement). Unions continued to push for wage gains that employers often had little choice but to concede, producing a self-reinforcing spiral of wage and price increases. The result was increasing pressure on the welfare state, and what came to be referred to as a 'legitimation crisis' (Habermas 1975). In this context, neoliberal approaches increasingly came to view public institutions of insurance and income provision as sources of problems since they provided people with non-market options of subsistence. Chapter 3 examines the resulting neoliberal transformations of work and welfare. The policy turn of the early 1980s unapologetically prioritized combating inflation over maintaining full employment, leading to an accelerated decline of the Fordist manufacturing sector. The result has been the rise of precarious employment, inconsistent access to public benefits accompanied by increased surveillance, and a growing reliance on financial services and debt. Under these circumstances, welfare has been transformed in qualitative ways: it is not simply that welfare benefits have been reduced, the welfare state has also become thoroughly imbricated with the restructured operations of the capitalist economy at large. This is evident in the growing reliance on 'activation' policies (Adkins 2012) – whereby the unemployed must participate in activities such as job-readiness programmes in order to qualify for welfare payments – and in the 'financialization' of welfare, whereby investors can invest in the efficient delivery of welfare schemes by buying 'impact bonds' (Schram 2015: ch. 7). The latter phenomenon has so far remained limited in quantitative terms, but it is indicative of the ways in which the boundaries between the public and the private have become blurred.

Corporations have been key agents in the neoliberal transformation of economic life, and their role is the focus of Chapter 4. The large industrial corporation was a key institution of the Fordist era, not simply fulfilling an economic function but also serving as a source of public regulation and social cohesion. This was especially clear in the US, where corporations often took on many of the insurance and welfare functions that in European countries were fulfilled by state institutions. We certainly should not idealize the role of the Fordist corporation during the early postwar era, but it provides a useful vantage point from which to assess the way in which the role of the corporation has changed in recent years. Whereas the Fordist corporation was at least to some extent set up to work in the interests of a wide variety of stakeholders (owners, managers, workers, customers, etc.), the neoliberal corporation is more singularly centred on profit and shareholder value. Changes in financial markets have been highly consequential here too: nowadays, any publicly listed firm suspected of not being managed efficiently will quickly face the threat of a hostile takeover (this is what the 'private equity' and 'mergers and acquisitions' sectors of the financial industry are all about). This does not mean, however, that corporations have been passive in relation to financial markets, or that neoliberalism has returned them to more purely economic functions. On the contrary, it has become abundantly apparent in the neoliberal era that corporations are sources of sovereignty (Barkan 2013). Few of us relate to large corporations as competing market actors – we know that they make and enforce the rules and that we as individuals do not command similar authority. Indeed, from the very start corporations have played an active role in disseminating the core ideas and practices of neoliberalism. Chapter 4 traces this political role of corporations in bringing neoliberal discourses to prominence, as well as their role in reorganizing patterns of exploitation, production and politics.

Chapter 5 draws together some of the lines traced in previous chapters by examining how the core institutional dynamics of neoliberal restructuring have combined to effect far-reaching changes in the operation of social power and the distribution of resources. It opens with a reflection on the way in which capitalism in general produces inequality, and returns to the question of how we should see the relationship between capitalism as a general category and neoliberalism. On the one hand, this book cautions against the tendency to see neoliberalism as a *sui generis* system, examined in isolation from the wider question of capitalism. On the other hand, as we have argued, neoliberalism is by no means a simple return to an older form of laissez-faire capitalism. We emphasize that neoliberalism needs to be understood as an attempt to reinvigorate capitalism, to rekindle its dynamism in a context where older mechanisms of exploitation and domination seem to have lost their viability. In this respect, neoliberalism has been a very successful project: it has reversed the trend whereby resistance from the lower classes constrained the power of capitalist elites, and the past decades have seen a tremendous increase in the growth of inequality. The growth of social and economic inequality has of course become a prominent theme since the financial crisis of 2007–8. Discourses denouncing the concentration of wealth in the hands of the '1%' are no longer at the margins of public life and have formed the basis for a great deal of political mobilization. Since the growth of inequality is a trend that dates back to the 1970s, the response to it has been rather delayed. The wider traction that such themes have found in recent years reflects above all the fact that even the middle class in Western countries is no longer exempt from the effects of such trends. In that sense, the neoliberal reconfiguration of power relations is not simply about material distribution but equally about the growth of insecurity. As many younger readers of this book will no doubt recognize, it is perfectly possible to have played by all the rules yet still be faced with the prospect of several decades of debt, inconsistent unemployment, and what appears to be the virtual impossibility of ever owning a home.

By the end of the book, the reader may wonder how we are still stuck with a system that is responsible for so much economic misery, produces constant instability, forces people into perennial competition, erodes the ability of political processes to reflect democratic priorities, and provokes so much discontent and criticism. Chapter 6 concludes the book by reflecting on some of the issues at stake. The end of neoliberalism has been announced many times. The crisis of 2007–8 was one of those moments: it may be hard to remember now, but for a little while following the onset of the crisis there was widespread optimism among progressively inclined commentators that neoliberalism had run its course and that a return to Keynesianism would be forthcoming without too much delay. Subsequent years have proven those predictions to be mistaken – indeed, neoliberalism has not simply survived but in many ways its reign has been consolidated, as has been evident with the turn to austerity in the wake of the crisis. Mainstream discourses have quickly become fascinated with the idea of resilience, as a distinct property of systems that will ensure their ability to bounce back from and even thrive amid instability. But there is no reason to believe that neoliberalism has found a magic wand that will ward off any and all threats. In other words, although this book cautions against the tendency to see the end of neoliberalism in each crisis, we should be equally wary of buying into a Hayekian fantasy of neoliberalism as a hyper-efficient and infallible system of self-organization (Connolly 2013). Neoliberalism will no doubt falter many more times, but it is unlikely that we will see the end of it until we come to terms with the ways in which it reproduces itself even through episodes and events that by any rational, dispassionate assessment would appear to signal its fundamental failure.

1
Neoliberalism in Historical Perspective

Before embarking on a more detailed investigation of the nature of neoliberalism with reference to some of its key institutions, in this chapter we will present a broad overview of its historical development. This is important not simply for the sake of completeness and to ensure a basic sense of historical orientation, but also because the question of periodization has assumed a central place in current debates on neoliberalism. For a long time – during the period when it was more a word than a concept – neoliberalism was typically understood to have had its starting point in the late 1970s and early 1980s, with the rise of Thatcher and Reagan. At the time, most scholarly attention was devoted to tracing the effects of the revolution in politics and policy they represented. Later this was supplemented with a closer examination of the decade that preceded the rise of Thatcher and Reagan. Of course it had always been understood that the revolutions they ushered in did not come out of nowhere, but scholars began to think of neoliberalism less as a discrete set of policies and more as a complex and multifaceted political phenomenon that needed to be traced with reference to the economic tensions, social changes and political struggles that had emerged from the 1960s onwards. Neoliberalism was now seen less as a clean reversal of an era of embedded liberalism or as a straightforward destruction of the Keynesian welfare state, and more as the contingent outcome of a series of institutionally situated contestations.

This interest in the (pre)history of neoliberalism has done a great deal to open up the scholarly field, transforming the notion of neoliberalism from a technical concept that preoccupied a limited number of critically minded political scientists into an interdisciplinary notion employed more widely to capture a much broader set of social changes. It was in this context that many scholars became increasingly interested in the intellectual precursors of contemporary neoliberalism. We have already discussed some of this work in the introduction, where we cautioned against the tendency (pronounced among recent contributions) to draw a straight line from the Mont Pelerin Society to the institutional structure of contemporary neoliberalism. As we have argued, the intellectual origins of neoliberalism are significant not primarily for their direct impact on actual political organization and strategies, but rather for the ways in which they formulate and articulate some of the distinctive rationalities of neoliberal governance. Indeed, neoliberal ideas were ignored for many years and eventually gained traction only thanks to a very specific set of circumstances.

Intellectual origins

In the introduction, we argued that the origins of a distinctly neoliberal way of thinking can be traced to the interwar period, and that some of its key concerns and ideas were articulated already in the socialist calculation debate. But it was only after the Second World War that such ideas were first allied to significant organizational efforts. In 1947, at the invitation of Friedrich Hayek, a small group of intellectuals gathered at the Hotel du Parc, on the slopes of Mont Pèlerin overlooking Lake Geneva in Switzerland, to discuss what they perceived as the growing threat to a free society posed by the rise of 'collectivism'. They were mostly economists, including Hayek, Milton Friedman, Ludwig von Mises and Lionel Robbins, but also included the well-known philosophers Karl Popper and Michael Polanyi (Cockett 1994;

Burgin 2012). At this meeting the Mont Pelerin Society was formed, which went on to be the nucleus of what grew into a global movement of neoliberal intellectuals and think tanks.

The neoliberals were united by a broad set of shared principles centred on the primacy of individual liberty and an understanding of the market as the enabler of such liberty, and by their identification of a common enemy. But there were also differences. Significant topics of disagreement concerned the proper role of the state within a market economy and the relationship between markets and democracy. Although the common characterization of neoliberalism in terms of its support for free markets is correct as far as it goes, it is crucial to appreciate these differences in regard to the proper role of the state, both quantitatively (how large can a state be, how much activity can it regulate and how many resources can it absorb through taxation?) and qualitatively (what kind of political and bureaucratic processes are consistent with a free market order?). Indeed, the first Mont Pelerin meeting was characterized by a considerable willingness to question the classic liberal commitment to non-intervention and laissez-faire.

Hayek at times had a quite expansive view of the role of the state in underpinning a free society. In *The Road to Serfdom*, for example, he argued that 'probably nothing has done so much harm to the liberal cause as the wooden insistence of some liberals on certain rough rules of thumb, above all the principle of *laissez-faire*' (1945: 29). The problem, he claimed, was that 'The range and variety of government action that is, at least in principle, reconcilable with a free system is thus considerable. The old formulae of laissez faire or non-intervention do not provide us with an adequate criterion for distinguishing between what is and what is not admissible in a free system' (2006: 202). Certainly, Hayek expressed a preference for the devolution of government functions to market relations, yet he was not an advocate of small government per se. Indeed, he argued that 'it is the character rather than the volume of government activity that is important. A functioning market economy presupposes certain activities on the part of the state; there are some other such activities by which its functioning will be assisted; and it can tolerate many more, provided that they are of the kind which are compatible with a functioning market' (2006: 194).

During the early years of his involvement, Friedman's position regarding the proper role of the state was quite close to that of Hayek. In a 1952 article titled 'Neoliberalism and Its Prospects' (interestingly, one of the few instances of a Mont Pelerin intellectual identifying himself with the term 'neoliberalism'), Friedman critiqued laissez-faire, arguing that it contained a 'basic error' because it 'failed to see that there were some functions the price system could not perform' and that, while interference in the activities of private individuals should be severely limited, 'there are important positive functions that must be performed by the state' (2012: 6–7). During the 1950s, however, Friedman began to advocate a much more consistently rigorous laissez-faire view (Burgin 2012), although he certainly still believed that the state had a necessary role to play in underpinning the functioning of markets. In *Capitalism and Freedom* he argued that the economic role of government should be limited to three functions: to create and enforce a set of rules for market conduct; to overcome 'neighbourhood effects' where markets are unable to charge people for their actions as they impact upon others (what are today called market 'externalities'), such as for the effects of pollution or the use of small suburban roads; and to act on 'paternalistic grounds' on behalf of those individuals who are either unable to recognize or to act on their own preferences (Friedman 2002: 27–34). Beyond these functions, state intervention was deemed illegitimate. Thus, where Hayek had argued that the crucial variable in bringing about the neoliberal utopia was not the volume but the character of state activity, Friedman clearly thought both were important. He advocated a radical reduction in the economic size of the state and, in 2002, at the height of the neoliberal era, argued that the advanced economies were still characterized by 'creeping socialism' (Friedman and Friedman 2002) because state expenditure had not been sufficiently reined in.

These positions can be seen as providing the coordinates within which neoliberal thought and practice have moved. But we should not be too quick to associate these positions with specific intellectual camps or individuals. Hayek's work, for instance, is in many ways a model of conceptual flexibility: although the passages quoted above testify to his willingness to assign the state a role in bringing about neoliberalism, much of his work is devoted to a rejection of the idea that there can be any coordination mechanisms other than the market – even going so far as to argue, during the 1970s, that the production of money should be fully denationalized and returned to the market (Hayek 1976a). Nor should we see this as simple intellectual inconsistency: in many ways it represents a flexibility that would later be key to neoliberalism's political strength.

Over time, the neoliberal thought collective came to solidify around three dominant intellectual influences: Austrian economics, the Chicago School, and public choice theory. Again, while there was congruence between the three, in aggregate they also contributed a certain flexibility and malleability to neoliberal doctrine.

Austrian economics centred on the work of Hayek and his teacher, Ludwig von Mises. It was founded on a strong anti-rationalist disposition, which entailed a deep scepticism regarding the ability of human reason to apprehend the complexity of social phenomena. This was at the heart of the Austrian position within the socialist calculation debate during the 1920s. Hayek and von Mises argued that efficient economic planning was impossible because it suppressed market prices which in a free market economy acted as information signals about the dispersed preferences of the many disparate buyers and sellers. Thus socialist planners were always destined to create gluts or shortages. This understanding of prices, information and the limits of human knowledge was also at the heart of the Austrian defence of free markets and its preference for the devolution of state functions to the private sector. Hayek (1973: 35–54) would later develop this into a theory of social and economic orders, distinguishing between 'taxis' – a deliberately constructed order, such as a state – and 'cosmos' – a spontaneous order that is the product not of design but of evolution, such as a market.

Much more clearly grounded in neoclassical economics was the current of thought emanating from the University of Chicago. From the 1950s a distinctive form of economic analysis was developed at Chicago, led by key neoliberal intellectuals such as Milton Friedman, George Stigler, Aaron

Director and Frank Knight. They took the foundational principles of neoclassical economics – rational, self-interested, utility-maximizing individuals, with stable preferences, interacting through equilibriating markets – and applied them to all areas of the economy and, increasingly, to broader social phenomena as well. The 'Chicago School', as it came to be characterized, displayed a normative preference for free markets and limited government, which was buttressed by, and which in turn also informed, the School's economic analysis (see Peck 2011). This approach reached its intellectual apogee in the work of Gary Becker, who argued that 'the economic approach is a comprehensive one that is applicable to all human behavior' (Becker 1990: 8), and that it should thus be applied 'unflinchingly' even to apparently non-economic phenomena, such as marriage, crime and addiction.

Meanwhile, at the University of Virginia, the foundational principles of neoclassical economics were being applied to political analysis in what became the third intellectual plank of neoliberalism: public choice theory. James Buchanan and Gordon Tullock felt that political analysis had for too long been hamstrung by the assumption that policymakers were benevolent and acted in the public interest. It seemed arbitrary and inconsistent to assume that people acted in one way in markets and another in politics. They therefore proposed that the basic methodological individualist tools of economic analysis should be applied to the political sphere, thereby treating all political agents (such as politicians and bureaucrats) as self-interested individuals seeking to maximize their utility. Politicians sought to maximize their votes, bureaucrats their departmental budgets. Also known as the 'economics of politics', it developed into a critique of the state that focused on the self-interested behaviour of policymakers who would tend to expand the size of government budgets (Buchanan et al. 1978). From this flowed two major policy conclusions. First, that the devolution of as many state functions as possible to the private sector is desirable, since markets are better able to respond to people's preferences than state officials. Second, that constitutional constraints should be put in place to curb government expenditure, such as rules mandating balanced budgets, or prohibiting deficits above a certain threshold.

In sum, the neoliberal vision of an ideal society entailed individuals being able to engage in market transactions free from third-party interference by governments, unions or other politically motivated entities or rules. In a world of voluntary transactions, self-interested individuals would not voluntarily enter into an agreement to their own disadvantage, and they were therefore free to pursue their own interests, creating a general protection of individual liberty. Moreover, markets, free from the regulatory privileges granted to special interests, also produced economically efficient outcomes, thereby guaranteeing a situation that was both economically desirable as well as moral, because it preserved individual liberty.

At the time the Mont Pelerin Society was formed, it would have been impossible to anticipate or foresee the political influence that neoliberal ideas would come to wield. Certainly, Hayek's *Road to Serfdom* had been a major bestseller. But as effective as his rhetorical denouncement of totalitarianism was, few took seriously his notion that there was a certain moral or political equivalence between Western social democracy and communism. Capital and labour had already hammered out a system to ensure the stability of capitalism, and that system was not neoliberalism but what has been called 'embedded liberalism' (Ruggie 1982), wherein private property and market regulation are complemented by extensive government intervention and planning, national ownership of key industries, and a range of programmes for public income provision. In terms of intellectual stature and influence on public policy, Hayek was dwarfed by Keynes. To be sure, we should be careful not to idealize the Keynesian system of the mixed economy as one that might function as a timeless model: it was a compromise between social forces, and although we tend to think of the postwar welfare state as providing workers with a degree of independence from the vagaries of the capitalist labour markets, it is equally important to appreciate that the system also functioned to blunt resistance and draw populations further into the dynamics of capitalism. This was certainly not lost on neoliberals, and we should be mindful here that German neoliberalism ('ordo-liberalism') advocated a reconstruction of capitalism along those very principles (what in Germany came to be called the 'social market economy').

The early postwar order and its decline

After the Second World War, a capitalist order emerged that was characterized by a much greater capacity to distribute its benefits and to integrate ordinary people into its dynamics; it consequently enjoyed a much higher degree of legitimacy. Western labour movements were strong, the threat of communism loomed large, and Western elites had become more concerned about the dangers of social instability and transformation. In this context, what emerged was a general sense that states were increasingly responsible for the welfare of their populations, which included not just maintaining full employment and economic growth but also the provision of a range of social services like housing, healthcare, education, etc. Keynesianism argued for a more active role for the state, which complemented well the ambition of social-democratic politics to extend political control over the economy.

Key here was the role of the US, which had emerged from the Second World War as the world's leading economic and military power. The US thus took responsibility for leading the reconstruction of capitalism in the war-ravaged economies of Western Europe and Japan, and deployed its military forces to police perceived threats to capitalism from socialist insurgencies across the globe. The postwar reconstruction was shaped by an acute awareness of the fact that American isolationism had been a major factor in the disintegration of the global economy during the interwar period. The concern was to avoid history repeating itself by designing institutions that would be capable of integrating different interests into the global economy. Central to this project was the creation of a system of fixed exchange rates that would shield countries from the destabilizing dynamics of speculative international finance.

By the 1960s these arrangements were unravelling. In particular, the US began to experience persistent balance of trade deficits, in part because of deteriorating manufacturing competitiveness but also because of the vast sums being poured into military expenditure for the war in Vietnam. These factors contributed to the US dollar being overvalued against gold, which led foreigners to cash in increasing amounts of dollars for gold, thus threatening a pillar of the international fixed exchange-rate system. In order to rebalance the system and restore faith in the gold value of the dollar, the US would have had to adopt a strategy of financial discipline. To avoid having to make such adjustments, the US state ended dollar convertibility altogether. On the evening of 15 August 1971, President Nixon made a televised address to the nation announcing the end of the convertibility of US dollars into gold. Although it was announced as a temporary measure, it meant the end of the fixed exchange-rate system under which the global economy had operated for the previous two and a half decades, during the so-called 'golden age' of capitalism, and a transition to a system of floating exchange rates (where the value of a currency is determined by the buying and selling of dollars in international money markets, rather than being set by state authorities according to agreed-upon targets) (Eichengreen 2008: 130–2; Ghizoni 2013). Under these circumstances, controls on flows of capital were increasingly less effective, and the US and other advanced capitalist states took a series of measures to deregulate their financial markets.

Floating exchange rates had of course been advocated by neoliberal intellectuals such as Milton Friedman (Silber 2012: 57–8, 105), because they reduced the direct influence of the state over price determination: in this case, the price of currency. Similarly, financial deregulation was advocated by neoliberals because it removed restrictions upon financial markets and private actors (especially corporations) who transacted in financial commodities. Fixed exchange rates and 'financial repression' (restrictions on the cross-border movement of capital) were viewed by neoliberals as hallmarks of Keynesian collectivism, and as threats not only to economic efficiency but to the liberal order more generally. In each case neoliberal theorists argued that freer markets, with fewer politically imposed constraints, would lead to a more efficient allocation of resources, and prices would better reflect people's preferences, leading to a healthier economy overall. Yet, while Friedman (who was an adviser to Nixon) and his fellow-travellers certainly played a role in these decisions, other factors were more important in driving such momentous changes. Chief among them was the desire of the US state to bolster its international power and loosen the constraints that the commitment to fixed exchange rates and capital controls had come to entail – and in this respect the Nixon policy shift was at least partly successful.

Advancing neoliberal policies

Rather than reflecting the direct influence of neoliberal ideas or representing a coherent political project, the shift to a new global financial regime created the conditions under which neoliberal conceptual templates could assume more distinctive organizational and ideological features. In the global North, the first regimes to put neoliberal forms of governance at the centre of their agenda were the conservative governments led by Margaret Thatcher, Prime Minister of Britain from 1979 to 1990, and Ronald Reagan, President of the US between 1981 and 1988. Neil Davidson (2010: 31) calls these 'regimes of reorientation' because each effected a radical neoliberal transformation of their national states. Older forms of economic and social regulation were 'rolled back' through deregulation and privatization, and new forms of neoliberal governance were 'rolled out' (Peck and Tickell 2002). Amid all of this, however, it is worth noting Dardot and Laval's reminder that 'The neo-liberal society we live in is the fruit of a historical process that was not fully programmed by its pioneers' (2013: 9). Neoliberalism as it developed in practice was the product of experimentation and institutionalized compromises in the context of crisis, as much as it was about a new vision of governance.

Many scholars have correctly noted that the first government for which neoliberalism became a central logic of economic regulation was the Pinochet dictatorship in Chile. On 11 September 1973, the elected government under the presidency of Salvador Allende was overthrown in a violent military coup by General Augusto Pinochet, who was secretly being backed by the US. Under Allende, the Chilean government had embarked on a social-democratic programme of nationalizing corporations in key industries, such as copper production and telecommunications, in which the US state had significant economic interests. After seizing power and murdering Allende, Pinochet repressed opposition to his authoritarian regime, killing, torturing and 'disappearing' thousands. Concurrently, he implemented a far-reaching programme of neoliberal economic restructuring, including privatization and deregulation. On economic issues Pinochet was advised by 'the Chicago Boys', a group of economists trained at the Chicago School, and similar neoliberal dictatorships followed in other Latin American countries such as Argentina. Yet Chile was more a harbinger of the violence neoliberalism was capable of than a template for the neoliberal revolution more generally. Indeed, democratically elected governments played a crucial role in promoting neoliberal policies.

When Thatcher was elected in 1979, unemployment and inflation were high and economic growth was low. This combination was dubbed 'stagflation', a set of conditions that bedevilled the advanced capitalist countries throughout the 1970s and early 1980s. The months preceding the 1979 election saw widespread strikes by public sector workers over wages, which were failing to keep pace with rapid inflation. It was dubbed 'The Winter of Discontent' by the conservative press, and the enduring image of the period was of bags of garbage piled up in city streets because council rubbish collectors were on strike. One of the election slogans of Thatcher's Tory Party, 'Labour isn't working', perfectly captured the sense of economic and social crisis and the inability of the incumbent Labour government to address either.

The Thatcher government radically transformed the British state and economy. One of the most significant transformations occurred through its privatization programme. Originally called 'denationalization', it entailed the sale of government assets to the private sector. The first major initiative in this process was the 1980 Housing Bill, known as the 'Right to Buy' policy, which enabled tenants in council houses to purchase them at a discounted rate (Steadman Jones 2012: 311–12; Bolick 1995: 542). Following this, between 1984 and 1987, major government-owned companies including British Telecom, British Gas, British Airways, Enterprise Oil, the British Airports Authority and the National Bus

Company were sold to private bidders, while others were partially privatized (Wolfe 1991: 248). State-owned water and electricity utilities followed in 1989 and 1990 (Wolfe 1991: 248–9). The Thatcher government's justification for privatization was that public ownership was inefficient, while private control was inherently superior as it subjected companies to the discipline of market competition. Yet in many cases these state-owned enterprises were made profitable by the government prior to their sale in order to make them more attractive to the market, which, as Gamble notes, 'meant that the Government was forced to authorize more public spending on precisely those programmes it most wanted to see cut' (1988: 104).

'Popular capitalism' was how Thatcher described this privatization process, arguing that by buying shares ordinary people now had a direct financial stake in, and control over, the commanding heights of the economy than was ever the case under the system of centralized government control of industry. While there was indeed a massive increase in share ownership flowing from privatization, this belied the significant concentration of large share-holdings remaining in the hands of a relatively small number of individuals and firms.

Thatcher was an admirer of key neoliberal intellectuals and close to the neoliberal think tanks such as the Institute of Economic Affairs. Indicative of this relationship, as noted in the introduction, was the letter she wrote to Hayek in 1979 soon after becoming Prime Minister, expressing the hope that his 'ideas will be put into practice by my Government' (Thatcher 1979). But it was not only in private correspondence that this close relationship was evident. Thatcher's public speeches were often infused with the discourse of radical neoliberalism, particularly in her focus on the virtues of the individual and the corrosive effects of the welfare state and 'big government'.

In practice, however, such rhetoric wasn't always matched by political reality. While government ownership of industry fell dramatically from 9 per cent to 4 per cent of GDP under Thatcher, the economic size of the state more generally remained remarkably stable, on average, during her prime-ministership. During the twelve years of 'Thatcherism', the average annual size of the state measured by expenditure as a proportion of GDP was 44.2 per cent, which is only marginally lower than the twelve years prior to her election when the average was 44.95 per cent (Guardian 2013). Savage cuts were certainly made to several areas of the budget, such as higher education. Funding to council services such as transportation was cut, prescription charges were increased and infrastructure spending delayed, all of which were felt disproportionately by lower-income earners. Concurrently, however, the government was pumping money into state-owned industries to make them profitable in the lead up to privatization, and the 'automatic stabilizers' of welfare payments further increased government expenditure as the ranks of the unemployed rose to 11.9 per cent in the deep recession of the early 1980s. Moreover, while deregulation was enacted across a range of key industries – including finance, telecommunications, transportation, gas and electricity – this also resulted in the creation of a host of new regulatory institutions, leading to a situation of concurrent market re-regulation. The power of central government also increased, becoming particularly evident in its interventions in the affairs of local councils, most strikingly represented by Thatcher's abolition of the Greater London Council.

One of the most iconic moments of Thatcher's tenure was her confrontation with the National Union of Miners (NUM) during the strike of 1984–5. The year-long miners' strike was a prolonged, violent and polarizing dispute that was highly significant for the implementation of Thatcher's neoliberal programme, but which also illuminates the key elements of neoliberalism more broadly. Thatcher viewed the weakening of trade union power as a key objective in and of itself, but also as crucial for the prosecution of her broader neoliberal agenda, to which the unions were likely to be opposed (Cockett 1994). The NUM was one of the more militant, left-wing unions, and since much of Britain's electricity and heating generation was dependent upon coal, it occupied a powerful position within the British economy. It was held responsible by many for the humiliating back-down by the Tory government during the 1973 coal strike, which provided the context for the Conservatives' subsequent electoral defeat. Thatcher was determined not to let this happen again. Prior to the strike, the government stockpiled coal so as to undermine the effect of union members withdrawing their labour, and effectively engineered a confrontation by announcing a series of closures of government-owned coal mines for being uneconomical, thereby provoking the union into calling a strike.

The government had to draw upon an enormous reservoir of resources to defeat the union, including thousands of police officers and the apparatuses of the secret service. Many towns in the North of England saw intense conflict between police and striking miners. After the bitter year-long dispute, which saw divisions within the union intensify under the pressure, the NUM was defeated and the miners returned to work. The significance of this went beyond the government's immediate victory, proving crucial for the neoliberal agenda more broadly. It presaged the later privatization of the mining industry under Thatcher's successor John Major, and led over the next two decades to a decimation of the industry in Britain. Moreover, Thatcher's confrontation with and defeat of one of the iconic institutions of working-class power made other unions wary of militant mobilizations, thus paving the way for further neoliberalization of the state and economy. This moment is emblematic of Gamble's (1988) description of the Thatcher era as one of 'the free economy and the strong state', a characterization that is instructive for an understanding of neoliberalism more generally and a key theme of this book as a whole.

One year after Thatcher became Prime Minister in Britain, Ronald Reagan was elected President of the US. Like Thatcher, he was close to fundamentalist neoliberal intellectuals – Milton Friedman, for example, was an economic adviser, and the Heritage Foundation, the leading US neoliberal think tank, found in the Reagan administration a sympathetic ear for its *Mandate for Leadership* (Heatherly 1981), a 3,000-page blueprint for neoliberalizing the US state and its regulation of the economy. In his public discourse, Reagan often gave a populist inflection to neoliberal ideas, as was evident in his inaugural presidential address:

> In this present crisis, government is not the solution to our problem; government is the problem...It is no coincidence

that our present troubles parallel and are proportionate to the intervention and intrusion in our lives that result from unnecessary and excessive growth of government...It is my intention to curb the size and influence of the Federal establishment...In the days ahead I will propose removing the roadblocks that have slowed our economy and reduced productivity. (Reagan 1981)

In practice, however, as in the early years of Thatcher's reign, government expenditure increased under the Reagan administration. Moreover, Reagan ran a persistent deficit on the US federal budget. As Modigliani notes:

> The most distinctive features [*sic*] of the Reagan administration economic policy is the enormous deficit which it ran continuously through its tenure of office. What makes it especially remarkable is that in the course of his campaign and early speeches Reagan had labeled the deficit public enemy number one, responsible for the supposed 'calamity' afflicting the U.S. economy. (1988: 407)

Certainly, Reagan cut funding to a range of social and welfare programmes targeted at low-income earners and the poor. Moreover, under Reagan, responsibility for many welfare programmes was transferred to the states, and, as Moody wrote at the time, 'the total amounts available to the states are reduced and the states often left with the job of implementing the cuts' (1987: 158). This bequeathed to the mostly Democrat-controlled state governments the problem of how to ration a reduced welfare budget, and many responded by tightening eligibility requirements. But whereas an austerity approach characterized the Reagan administration's regulation of the poor, military expenditure was simultaneously ramped up (a move labelled by some as 'military Keynesianism' because of the stimulus it gave to consumption and investment) and both corporate and personal income tax rates were cut. The increase in military expenditure funded what some at the time called a 'new' or 'second' Cold War. This entailed a more aggressive stance towards the Soviet Union, both rhetorically and militarily. The Reagan administration also armed and supported state terrorism against left-wing and other resistance movements abroad, such as in Guatemala, and supported armed insurgency against left-wing governments, such as in Nicaragua.

Like Thatcher, Reagan also took action against organized labour. The best-known example of this was the Professional Air Traffic Controllers Organization (PATCO) dispute, in which the government took an uncompromising approach towards the union, sacking the 13,000-strong workforce, and jailing its leading activists. These actions sent a clear message that the administration would not be sympathetic to striking workers – a message underlined by a series of anti-labour appointments made by Reagan to the National Labor Relations Board. The combination of the appointees' judicial activism and the fact that many labour disputes were left unattended helped to facilitate a strengthening of managerial prerogatives and a decline in union influence within workplaces across the country. Thus Reagan's neoliberalism in practice entailed not only a transformation of the state but also an aggressive strategy of confrontation against centres of organized opposition to the prerogatives of US corporations, at home or overseas, and to the expansion of neoliberal capitalism more generally.

There is a tendency in much of the literature to take the Reagan and Thatcher governments as exemplars of neoliberalism, and therefore to treat these early moves towards a neoliberal agenda as a phenomenon specific to governments from the right of the political spectrum. Important though such governments were in establishing a new direction in economic management globally, such a view ignores other contemporaneous governments that were in the vanguard of neoliberal change in the 1980s, but which were from the centre-left. Indeed, it often goes unnoticed by scholars that these followed earlier steps down the path to neoliberalism taken by centre-left governments that *preceded* the Thatcher and Reagan regimes. The Democratic President Jimmy Carter, for example, pioneered a neoliberal agenda with his deregulation of the airlines, trucking, railroads and oil prices. Carter also appointed Paul Volcker as Chairman of the Federal Reserve Board, thus paving the way for what many have termed the use of 'monetarist' policies (popularized by Milton Friedman) to fight inflation. Likewise, in the mid to late 1970s in Britain, the centre-left Labour government led by James Callaghan

introduced a number of measures that look remarkably neoliberal, including selling off part of the state's stake in British
Petroleum, thus initiating the privatization programme that
was so central to Thatcher's economic strategy. With respect
to centre-left governments contemporaneous with Thatcher
and Reagan, the Labor governments in Australia and New
Zealand and the French Socialist government under President François Mitterrand all undertook wide-ranging programmes of neoliberal restructuring in the 1980s (Humphrys
and Cahill 2016).

Spreading neoliberalism

From the mid-1980s, as neoliberalism was being rolled out by
such governments in the global North, a profound neoliberal
transformation of states and economies was also occurring
across the global South, where the anti-democratic tendencies of neoliberal restructuring were often much more pronounced. Led by the International Monetary Fund, structural
adjustment programmes (SAPs) began to be imposed upon
heavily indebted states within developing economies. Such
programmes gave indebted states access to further credit with
which to service their debts, but in return for a radical neoliberal restructuring that included the deregulation of finance
and trade as well as the privatization of public assets.

SAPs were introduced in 1985 via the 'Baker Plan', named
after James Baker, the US Treasury Secretary during the
Reagan presidency (Chorev and Babb 2009). The context
was the debt crisis that had eroded the public finances of
many developing countries in the early 1980s. In the previous
decade the governments of developing economies were able
to secure relatively easy access to credit because the major
global banks were looking for outlets for the massive cash
surpluses accruing to oil-exporting states as a consequence
of the high price of oil. However, the combination of global
recession and the steep rise in global interest rates, led by
the previously mentioned 'Volcker shock', undermined the
ability of developing countries to repay their loans. Baker, as

representative of the US state – which controlled the largest share of votes on the governing board of the IMF and which, together with other advanced capitalist states, formed a dominant voting bloc – stepped in to broker a series of loans from private sector financiers that would be administered by the IMF. The conditions included the privatization of public assets, the deregulation of capital markets and trade, and cuts to rates of corporate and personal income tax (Chorev and Babb 2009: 468–9). Prior to this, the very rationale of the IMF had been under threat, since it had been set up to support the fixed exchange-rate system established as a pillar of the postwar economic order, a system which, as discussed, was collapsing by the mid-1980s. The Baker Plan thus gave the IMF a new lease of life as an institution for rolling out a neoliberal agenda across the global South. It provided the template for the conditionality attached to IMF loans into the next decade: between 1986 and 2000 the IMF approved the use of its structural adjustment or 'enhanced structural adjustment' facilities for 131 programmes across fifty countries (Barro and Lee 2002; IMF 2004). This was a key factor in the exporting of neoliberalism from the global North to the global South.

In the early 1990s, a series of seismic political events shook the world and had profound ramifications for the development of neoliberalism. A combination of popular social movements and severe economic shortages led to the collapse of those communist states under the influence of the Soviet Union. One-by-one, the Eastern European states, and the Soviet Union itself, replaced state-socialism with neoliberal-style capitalism. It is difficult to overestimate the magnitude of this transformation. Price controls were abolished and a massive privatization programme saw over 150,000 large and medium-sized enterprises, and many more small businesses and dwellings, transferred to private ownership across the former communist states. As Aslund argues, 'the world had never seen anything like this expansion of private enterprise' (2013: 191). The immediate effects were economically disastrous (Hamm, King and Stuckler 2012: 296). GDP collapsed across most of the states, and unemployment skyrocketed. In Russia, for example, which had among the harshest experiences of neoliberalization, GDP in 1999 was at 57 per cent of its level a decade prior (Aslund 2013: 66–8; Sokol 2001: 648). Life expectancy also declined in many post-communist countries, due to factors such as malnutrition, suicide and alcoholism, as people were subject to new market discipline (Aslund 2013: 222; Gowan 1999: 204).

This process was labelled 'shock therapy' because it involved rapid and radical change to the very structure of the former communist economies. As the Harvard economist Jeffrey Sachs, one of the architects of shock therapy, argued at the time in an article titled 'What Is to Be Done?' (1990), the transition to a market economy should 'be decisive and rapid'. The title of Sachs' article is a deliberate allusion to a pamphlet of the same name by Lenin, leader of the 1917 Bolshevik revolution in Russia which had created the communist state-system now being dismantled by Sachs and the governments he advised and inspired. The title captures something of the triumphalism which greeted the collapse of communism. Thatcher's dictum that 'there is no alternative' to neoliberalism seemed to be borne out by the events in Eastern Europe as the neoliberal agenda continued its seemingly inexorable colonization of states and parties from left to right across the globe. With the implosion of what was widely perceived to be its only significant existing alternative, the legitimacy of capitalism was given a major boost, as was its neoliberal expression.

Perhaps less noticed at the time, but at least as significant, was the neoliberalization of the Chinese state and economy. Here, the process had begun earlier, in 1978, and was pursued more gradually, but it nonetheless brought about a profound transformation of the still nominally communist country. Beginning with the introduction of competition between state-owned companies, production for profit in the agricultural sector, and the opening up of the economy to foreign trade and capital, by the early twenty-first century China's communist government had embarked upon a massive privatization programme. As Harvey writes, the effect was 'the construction of a particular kind of market economy that increasingly incorporates neoliberal elements interdigitated with authoritarian centralized control' (2005: 120).

Consolidating neoliberalism

By the 1990s, neoliberalism had become a dominant policy norm in many countries. Of course, there was significant unevenness to this process, and some of the early adopting states had experienced more extensive neoliberalization than others. Nonetheless, most states around the world, whether authoritarian or democratic, and irrespective of the political hue of the governing party, had embraced deregulation and privatization, some form of floating currency, and income and corporate tax cuts. In the consolidation phase, these processes continued, but efforts were also made to extend them into new areas such as welfare and the natural environment. With respect to the latter, for example, not only were natural resources such as land and water commodified in many countries through privatization, market mechanisms were also justified as a way of conserving nature, as can be seen in the development of various 'carbon trading' schemes selling permits to pollute, which can then be on-sold, in an attempt to use the price mechanism to stimulate the development of less-polluting forms of production and the use of existing resources more efficiently. Thus, from the 1990s, neoliberalism increasingly became what some scholars label a 'rationality' of state (Davies 2014; Foucault 2008), meaning that neoliberal norms came to underpin how bureaucrats carried out policies, as well as the forms those policies took. New public management, for example, whereby the public sector is reshaped according to forms of evaluation borrowed from the private sector, is one important example evident in many capitalist states.

This process of embedding neoliberal forms of calculation more deeply within the apparatuses of the state, effectively pre-committing states to neoliberal policies, was also ensured by governments signing up to supra-national organizations such as the World Trade Organization and the European Union, which had neoliberal principles at their heart. The WTO was founded in 1994 during the Uruguay Round of negotiations over the General Agreement on Tariffs and Trade, itself an artefact of the earlier postwar era of global economic regulation. Whereas the GATT was focused primarily on tariff reductions, the purview of the WTO was extended to cover intellectual property and services more generally (Chorev and Babb 2009). As well as enforcing the monopoly rights of intellectual property owners (such as multinational agribusiness or pharmaceutical companies), the WTO also requires member states to reduce both tariff and non-tariff barriers to trade, potentially undermining the ability of governments to enact social and environmental protections if these are seen as undermining free trade. Many 'free trade' agreements signed between states also share such features.

The EU, formally founded in 1993 but with a much longer gestation period, is similarly 'structurally biased towards policies of neoliberal restructuring' (Van Apeldoorn 2009: 6). The chief reason for this is the institutional arrangements at the heart of the European Monetary Union (EMU), which began in a practical sense in 1999 when member states replaced their national currencies with the euro. Under the Maastricht Treaty, which led to these profound changes, the budget deficits of member states were not permitted to rise above 3 per cent of GDP and government debt could not exceed 60 per cent of GDP. Moreover, responsibility for monetary policy was removed from individual member states and placed in the hands of the newly formed European Central Bank, the focus of which was on maintaining low inflation. Such structural biases would become evident during the sovereign debt crisis in Europe from 2010 onwards, when harsh austerity conditions were imposed on the governments of Greece, Portugal and Spain. Beyond this, however, the EU has created a Europe-wide legal framework that privileges neoliberalism, for example by making it more difficult to exclude private capital from the delivery of social services. This is part of a global trend towards the enactment of a competition policy which effectively institutionalizes neoliberal principles such as the private provision of social services and the refusal to subsidize state entities in order to give them a competitive market advantage over private providers. In each of these cases 'national interest' provisions allow states, under some circumstances, to circumvent neoliberal principles in favour, for example, of public provision or the quarantining of natural resources from private exploitation for profit. But the main function of such institutions is to pre-commit governments, irrespective of political hue, to neoliberalism. Such processes have been labelled as forms of neoliberal 'constitutionalism' (Gill 2016) and 'de-democratization'.

This institutional embedding of neoliberalism is also evident in transformations of fiscal and monetary policy. Constitutional limitations on the ability of governments to run deficits, or mandating that they produce balanced budgets, has long been a goal of neoliberal intellectuals, especially those from the 'Virginia' or public choice school. By the early twenty-first century a range of rules constraining government fiscal policy had been enacted in various capitalist states. From the 1970s in the US, for example, many states and municipalities became subject to tax and expenditure limitations, which significantly curtailed their fiscal freedom (Waisanen 2010). This occurred in a context in which 'direct outlays to municipalities were slashed' and local governments became tasked with new obligations (Hackworth 2007: 24–6). As a result, such governments increasingly used private debt to finance their operations, turned to various forms of public-private partnership, and introduced new competitive arrangements such as vouchers into the delivery of public services. In the sphere of monetary policy too, various constraints have been institutionalized. Although again there is an unevenness to the process, Saad-Filho (2007: 90) sees the combination of rules-based inflation-targeting and central bank independence as part of the 'new monetary policy consensus' of contemporary neoliberalism. Once again, the clear effect is that governments become constrained in their room for manoeuvre, thus locking in forms of neoliberal policy irrespective of political ideology.

Indeed, during this consolidation phase, it was centre-left governments just as much as those from the right that rolled out neoliberalism. In the US, for example, it was Democratic President Bill Clinton who in 1993 signed the North American Free Trade Agreement (NAFTA) into law, creating a free trade zone between Canada, Mexico and the US. In 1996 Clinton also supported the Personal Responsibility and Work Opportunity Reconciliation Act (PRWORA), a pioneering bill which transformed welfare provision from being an entitlement of citizenship into something one only receives on the condition of performing work and other activity tests.

This pushed people into typically low-paid, precarious work by setting time limits and making the receipt of assistance more onerous. The bill had radical implications for the unemployed and underemployed in the US, but it also served as an example to other political leaders of new ways to regulate the poor.

Centre-left governments in other leading capitalist states also embraced forms of neoliberal policy. In Britain the Labour Party, during its long period of parliamentary opposition in the 1980s and 1990s, gradually embraced key elements of the Thatcher government's economic agenda. Under the leadership of Tony Blair it rebranded itself as 'New Labour' in an attempt to signal a rejection of the party's socialist heritage and an embrace of a modern yet compassionate approach to government. After its election victory in 1997, Blair's New Labour set about implementing its 'new deal' unemployment policy – a workfarist approach compelling the unemployed to undertake work, training and interviews as a condition of receiving government support – even as it boosted public spending directed at economically disadvantaged groups. These policy combinations led Jessop (2003: 2) to describe the New Labour period (1997–2010) as 'Thatcherism with a Christian socialist face'. In Germany too, the centre-left Social Democratic Party (SPD) came to embrace neoliberalism. In 2002, for example, it privatized the state-run employment agency and tightened eligibility requirements for unemployment assistance, while also cutting benefits. Such centre-left parties styled themselves as part of a new 'third way' between capitalism and state-socialism, yet, while they often distanced themselves from the hard-edged policies of Thatcher and Reagan, and while their rhetoric was far less strident, Callinicos is surely right to conclude that 'far from breaking with the neoliberal policies of the new right ... [they] continued and, in certain ways, radicalized them' (2001: 121). Similarly, in South Africa, the left-wing African National Congress, which has governed continuously since 1994, has substantially neoliberalized the state and economy. The country has experienced privatization, deregulation, cuts to corporate tax rates, and the erosion of protections for domestic industries, and has laboured under IMF loan conditionalities (Bond 2014).

Neoliberalism into the twenty-first century

Perhaps not surprisingly, these neoliberal transformations have generated significant opposition and resistance. There are myriad examples across the world of organized protest against particular policies. For example, Walton and Seddon (1994: 39–40) document 146 protests across developing countries from 1976–1992 in response to austerity and structural adjustment. We are not aware of a similar global aggregate, but it seems likely that a count of the incidences of collective action against neoliberalism across the world from the 1970s to the present, inclusive of protests against deregulation, user-pays schemes, privatizations, land commodification and free trade agreements, would easily number in the tens of thousands. While dissent against neoliberalism has been a recurrent feature of the era as a whole, it was during the consolidation phase that it became a transnational phenomenon. The first real public awareness of this came during the World Trade Organization meeting at Seattle in 1999, when tens of thousands of trade unionists, environmentalists, indigenous groups and third-world solidarity activists converged on the city in an attempt to shut down the meeting. They were protesting against what the WTO represented – free trade, the rights of corporations over citizens, de-democratization and privatization – as much as against what it actually did. Repressed violently by the city police, images of the Seattle protests were beamed around the world by the news media, and through the burgeoning 'indy-media' sources.

While presented by the mainstream news media as coming out of the blue, in reality the Seattle protests built upon and emerged out of earlier transnational protests against key institutional agents of neoliberalism – such as the global protests to mark the fiftieth anniversary of the World Bank, and the movement which resulted in the abandonment of the Multilateral Agreement of Investment (MAI), which was an attempt to construct a set of global rules for trade structured around neoliberal norms. After Seattle, similar types of protest came to be repeated at the meetings of key supranational institutions – such as the IMF, G7/8, and the WEF – the world over. Bringing together activists with a range of agendas and ideologies, this was, as Klein (2001) argues, a 'movement of movements'. Moreover, while most participants identified it as being against 'globalization', it was also through this movement that the term 'neoliberal' gained much greater currency as the descriptor of what was being opposed. For decades 'neoliberalism' had been used by the Latin American left to describe the process of state restructuring centred on privatization, deregulation and the repression of opposition from the Pinochet regime onwards (Boas and Gans-Morse 2009); the rise of the anti-globalization movement in 1999 provided a vehicle for the transfer of this discourse to Northern activists and, indeed, academics. Ultimately, the anti-globalization movement would merge with the anti-war movement which opposed the US-led invasions of Afghanistan and, especially, Iraq, where a new form of neoliberal shock therapy was imposed by the US state. Far from being confined to the metropoles of the richer nations, however, some of the most hard-edged and mass-based mobilizations against neoliberalism have continued to take place in the global South. In the 'Arab Spring' of 2011, for example, ostensibly pro-democracy movements in countries including Egypt, Libya, Tunisia and Iraq were often also protesting against the corruption and nepotism, actual or perceived, associated with privatizations and PPPs introduced by the ruling authoritarian regimes, or against economic inequality and the unaffordability of basic foodstuffs attributed to processes of liberalization (Achar 2013: 53–4; Hourani 2014).

But even though the past decade and a half has seen a series of significant challenges to the hegemony of neoliberalism, we should recognize that it has also displayed a remarkable ability to ward off, defuse and placate political opposition or otherwise incorporate it into its own dynamics. Amid what seemed to be a backlash against economic deregulation and globalization, the Bush administration came to power in the US on a programme that brought neoliberalism into an alliance with neoconservative ideas and policies. Many progressive commentators have expressed a great deal of frustration over the willingness of 'value-voters' to support a political programme that was so clearly at odds with their economic interests. But as much as the Obama administration subsequently positioned itself in ideological opposition to neoconservatism, there can be little doubt that it was also a highly reliable steward of neoliberal capitalism. The global financial crisis, which broke out the year before President Obama's election, was widely seen as signalling the end of neoliberalism, as it generated not just intense economic instability but also widespread political mobilization and opposition. A decade on, however, it appears that the Obama administration above all managed that insecurity and discontent in ways that have contributed to the reproduction of neoliberal capitalism. From the start, many expressed concern that Obama's commitment to traditionally progressive ideals and policy goals was lacklustre, but the fact that for much of his presidency Obama was forced to work with a Congress that was unsympathetic at best and obstructionist at worst did a great deal to further limit the political possibilities. The perception that eight years under a nominally progressive President failed to reverse the trend of growing inequality was a major factor in the election of Donald Trump, whose victory has confused most of the categories that political analysts typically rely on to describe political constellations. Whether Trump represents a continuation of neoliberalism, its last gasp, or the start of something much more sinister altogether, must remain an open question for the time being.

2
Neoliberal Finance

The expansion of finance has been one of the most prominent aspects of the neoliberal era. And it has been a particular concern for the *critics* of neoliberalism. It has of course hardly gone unnoticed by its supporters, but they have typically seen the growth of financial markets as simply one part of a broader movement of marketization that has beneficially transformed a wide range of economic sectors. Among more critically inclined commentators, however, the growth of finance has always occupied a central place. The reason for this is that there seems to be something essentially unsustainable about the proliferation of paper and electronic tokens of wealth in the absence of a corresponding growth in the real economy: it does not lead simply to economic conditions that are problematic or objectionable from a moral point of view, but creates economic conditions and policies that are seen as fundamentally incoherent. For instance, one can criticize the deregulation of labour markets for the ways in which it has negative effects on economic security, and one can criticize tax cuts for the way they promote inequality and fail to generate their 'trickle-down' effects. But the expansion of finance seems problematic in a more fundamental sense: that the growth of a huge pyramid of paper and fictitious money is unsustainable would seem to be a matter of simple logic.

In a sense, the growth of finance is seen as turning the world upside-down: instead of real economic production shaping monetary and financial relations, finance is perceived to have taken on a life of its own – it has become a case of the tail wagging the dog (Strange 1998; Hudson 2014).

Such criticisms of course capture something important about the character of neoliberal finance. Basic numbers here speak volumes. The Bank for International Settlements (2016) reports that in April 2016 the total volume of foreign transactions was $5.1 trillion per day – this should be seen in the context of a total global GDP of $73.5 trillion for the whole of 2015 (World Bank 2016). Similarly, global derivatives markets in 2013 amounted to $774 trillion, which represented a six-fold increase from 1998 (Bush 2016: 127). Such numbers indicate that there is something clearly 'disproportional' about the growth of finance: only the most tautological definition of productivity could maintain that all this financial activity is useful and conducive to the production of real wealth.

But the standard story may also be somewhat one-sided: we have been offered such seemingly absurd numbers for many years, and yet neoliberal finance has failed to crumble under the weight of its own contradictions. This chapter will therefore seek to complicate the received critical story somewhat. The point here is certainly not to defend or rehabilitate the idea that the expansion of financial markets is simply a sign of growing economic efficiency or a healthy engine of balanced growth. However, by focusing so strongly on its unsustainable character, the heterodox critique of the neoliberal financial system has been relatively weak when it comes to offering explanations for its persistent refusal to collapse. Critical scholarship has, for instance, been good at predicting crises, but much less adept at explaining the capacity of finance to resurrect itself in the wake of such crises. This speaks to the question of resilience, which we will look at more closely in Chapter 6. This chapter will discuss the key events and processes that compose modern finance, review some of the perspectives that have emerged to account for its growth in recent decades, and locate finance as a central component of neoliberalism.

Globalizing finance

As we discussed in Chapter 1, the closing of the gold window by President Nixon in 1971 stands as one of the iconic moments in the rise of neoliberalism. In order to understand the events leading up to this, we need to take account of the position of the US dollar during the preceding decades. After the Second World War the US had emerged as the main international power, and its currency had come to occupy a central position in the international payments system. The dollar's centrality gave the US access to the benefits of 'seignorage': the ability to make money simply by printing it (a benefit that was not available to, say, Sweden, as its currency did not function as international money). During the 1960s, the US began to make more and more use of what French President Charles de Gaulle referred to as this 'exorbitant privilege', not least to fund the escalating costs of the Vietnam War. This meant that the US was exporting large amounts of dollars abroad, which had come to form offshore pools that became the basis of the 'Eurodollar' markets. As the competitiveness of the American manufacturing sector began to weaken, foreigners started to wonder about the wisdom of holding US dollars and began to exchange their holdings for gold (Odell 1982). The result was a drain on American gold reserves. The US government thus decided to 'close the gold window', that is, to suspend the convertibility of the dollar into gold. Several years later it made this measure permanent and declared that it would let the dollar float.

The upshot of these developments was a transition from a regime of fixed exchange rates to a regime of floating exchange rates. The design of the postwar international monetary order had been deeply influenced by the experience of the interwar period, when currency speculation had wrought a great deal of havoc on the world economy; the architects of the Bretton Woods system were thus centrally concerned to limit the opportunities for destabilizing currency speculation (Helleiner 1994). A key step here had been the creation of a regime of fixed exchange rates, whereby currencies were pegged to the US dollar, which was convertible into gold. The Bretton Woods institutions – above all the IMF – were founded as organizations meant to support this regime, helping individual countries to manage the imbalances of currency supply and demand that are likely to emerge in a situation where price adjustments are not permitted. Taken together, and in combination with significant financial aid (e.g., the Marshall Plan), the Bretton Woods arrangements ensured that European countries would enjoy sufficient stability to be able to both rebuild their economic and social infrastructures and to construct the kind of institutions that would secure political legitimacy and so blunt the threat posed to capitalism by radical labour movements and communist ideology (Hogan 1987).

The US decision to allow the dollar's exchange rate to be determined by the forces of supply and demand was a way of allowing the value of the dollar to depreciate, rather than suffering a severe drain on its gold reserve. But this decision removed one of the key pillars of the postwar regime, and the new pressures of deregulated international finance made themselves felt in short order. The volume of international financial transactions began to increase dramatically, resulting in considerable financial volatility. When assessing such developments, we should not be too quick to portray this, as is often done, in terms of the unleashing of financiers' 'animal spirits', which tends to suggest a view of finance as a sort of pathology. It is of course true that many financiers will actively seek out and exploit opportunities for speculation, but it is equally important to appreciate that the transition to a market-based regime of international finance imposes a certain structural imperative to speculate. Even if one has little appetite for adventure and is primarily concerned to defend the value of a given portfolio of assets, the absence of an objective anchor of value means that investors are continuously adjusting their portfolios, very quickly generating large trading volumes and amplifying minor fluctuations into large oscillations, necessitating yet further rebalancing (Grahl and Lysandrou 2006).

In other words, speculation is not always an irrational impulse: in a context where correct prices ('fundamental values') are not known, some degree of speculation is bound to mark any investment decision. In this way, currency markets are driven by continuous assessments of whether particular currencies are overvalued or undervalued (assessments that were far less necessary under a regime of fixed exchange rates) (Bryan and Rafferty 2006). Moreover, such dynamics are often contagious: market actors do not necessarily simply guess at the 'real' value; they assess which currencies or assets are mispriced with reference to what they think other market actors think or feel (Bryan and Rafferty 2013), and sometimes this leads to what is known as 'herd behaviour'. For instance, speculation against a currency can have a self-reinforcing quality not for any objective reasons, but because investors see others selling and want to get out of their position before the currency value falls further.

States and financial markets

The decline of the international financial arrangements of the early postwar era created a very new environment for national states. Whereas before they had been able to conduct domestic policy without being subject to external pressures, they now became exposed to the logic of global finance. This meant that doubts about a country's economic competitiveness and its ability to sustain payments on its debts could very quickly translate into pressure on that country's currency, forcing it to take measures to improve its payments position in order to stave off further speculation against its currency. Increasingly, the operation of international financial markets worked at odds with the ability of states to maintain socially protective institutions, forcing them to use their policy instruments to instead enforce compliance with market forces.

One of the first major clashes between a national government and the new rule of international finance occurred in 1976, when speculation against sterling produced an acute crisis. The British government was forced to apply for a large loan from the IMF, which now took quite a different approach to the problem than it had in the past, making the loan conditional on the government's willingness to implement a domestic austerity programme that involved large cutbacks on public spending. The Labour government had been voted into office only two years earlier and had been committed to maintaining (and, indeed, extending) some of the key institutions of the postwar compromise. But the strings attached to the IMF loan subverted the policy auton- omy that was required for the continuation of such social- democratic policies (Harmon 1997). Following the effective end of the Bretton Woods system, the status of the IMF and the World Bank had become very uncertain, and their survival as relevant international bodies was contingent on their ability to reinvent themselves. Increasingly, instead of assisting countries with the management of their external position in ways that promoted domestic policy autonomy, both institutions – dominated by US interests – became key enforcers of the 'discipline' of global finance (Felder 2008). The 1976 British bailout presaged much of what was to come during the neoliberal era. Countries whose financial health and economic competitiveness were considered to be in doubt became subject to currency speculation, forcing them to seek funds from the IMF in exchange for promises to cut state budgets and neoliberalize economic regulations more generally.

We should not, however, think of this exclusively in terms of national states vs. international financial markets, as if this was a purely external relationship (Panitch 2000). The tensions at work here found expression within national states themselves, with different interests favouring different courses of institutional adjustment. For instance, the 1976 Labour government had come into power with a promise to maintain such key institutions as full employment and the welfare state. But the fact that its hands were tied by the terms of the IMF loan meant that it had difficulty following through on these promises, and became an active agent in managing the austerity that the loan initially opposed (Burk and Cairncross 1992). In particular, it became embroiled in an increasingly fraught relationship with the unions, who had traditionally been Labour allies but were now at odds with the government's policies, which relied increasingly on wage controls (Coates 1980). These tensions came to a head in the 'Winter of Discontent' of 1978–9, when the government was unable to prevent a long series of strikes by increasingly militant public sector unions (Hay 1996). In this context, the unions came to appear as representing a set of 'special interests' that the Labour Party had difficulty controlling in a way that was consistent with the national interest. These events played a major role in shifting electoral support from Labour to the Conservatives, and enabled Margaret Thatcher to marshal political and ideological support for the pro- gramme of neoliberal restructuring that she would implement once in office. Whereas Labour had reluctantly acquiesced to external pressure, Thatcher embraced it with open arms.

Inflation and the Volcker shock

One issue that assumed particular prominence under these circumstances was that of inflation. The kind of Keynes- ian theories and economic policies that had been prominent during the early postwar period saw a certain degree of infla- tion as an unobjectionable effect of fiscal stimuli that served to push up employment levels. But in many Western coun- tries during the 1970s inflation began to run at double-digit rates. Once economic actors began to anticipate inflation, they started to build this into contracts, creating a dynamic of self-fulfilling expectations and setting in motion an accel- erating inflation. The power of the unions to enforce the indexation of wages to inflation was of course crucial here. High and accelerating levels of inflation entailed a degree of uncertainty that was problematic for the everyday conduct of economic life, as it became impossible to know what one's dollar would be worth one year later. 'New classical' economic theories (e.g., Lucas 1976) now asserted that any beneficial effects that expansionary fiscal policies might have on levels of employment were limited and fleeting, and that beyond that they simply resulted in rising levels of inflation that caused general economic malaise, including rising unem- ployment. In this context, unions were increasingly portrayed as the enemies of full employment. As the British Prime Min- ister James Callaghan famously put it in 1976:

> We used to think that you could spend your way out of a recession and increase employment by cutting taxes and boosting government spending. I tell you in all candour that

that option no longer exists, and in so far as it ever did exist, it only worked on each occasion since the war by injecting a bigger dose of inflation into the economy, followed by a higher level of unemployment as the next step. (Quoted in Burton 2016: 9)

In the US, the Carter administration was also faced with runaway inflation (Biven 2014). This was a problem for the domestic economy, but also for the international position of the US. Although floating the dollar had been part of an attempt to gain some leeway in relation to external financial pressures, by the end of the decade the dollar became subject to serious speculative pressure, raising the prospect that the US might have to turn to the IMF cap-in-hand, much like the fallen imperial power that was the UK. Even the world's leading economy was not immune to the flows of international capital, and consequently there was tremendous pressure on Carter to control inflation. The discourse employed by Reaganism, while also inflected by the conservative ideologies to which American neoliberalism has always been allied, followed a similar logic to Thatcher's, promising a return to the common-sense free market values of entrepreneurialism and hard work, and the removal of the obstacles in the way of those ideals, above all cumbersome state regulations, taxes and unions. Inflation, in this logic, was what you get from handing out too many free lunches.

But things were already in motion by the time Reagan came into office. Carter had appointed Paul Volcker, who was known as a highly pragmatic public servant without strong ideological inclinations, as Chairman of the Federal Reserve. Soon after his appointment, Volcker announced a significant shift in the way the Federal Reserve would conduct its policies (Greider 1987). Although he did not set too much store by the intellectual value of the monetarist ideas that were then in ascendance (most prominently associated with Milton Friedman), he nonetheless felt that they would be helpful in legitimating the policies that needed to be implemented. Volcker announced that the Federal Reserve would aim to keep constant the overall level of reserves in the banking system, which determine the amount of credit that can be created and so the level of the money supply. The strength of this doctrine was that it drew some kind of line in the sand. During the 1960s and the 1970s, the Federal Reserve had become more concerned with the level of inflation, but combating inflation had remained one among a number of different objectives, which also included ensuring the flow of credit to industry, full employment, and promoting or stabilizing the demand for government debt. That is, monetary policy sought to establish a balance among different objectives, with explicit attention to the real economy and social objectives. This now changed dramatically: a constant price level became an unconditional objective around which other variables would be allowed to fluctuate (Clarke 1988). The shift to monetarism meant that the Federal Reserve would push interest rates up to whatever level would be required in order to stop the money supply from growing.

Debt and austerity

The most immediate effect of the Volcker shock was accordingly a dramatic increase in interest rates, which moved into double digits and for some time were close to 20 per cent. The effects of this were felt across the world, and were most dramatically manifest in the emergence of an international debt crisis. We should see this against the background of historical developments during the previous decades, when Southern countries sought to emancipate themselves from dependence on imports from the industrialized world through 'import-substitution' strategies aimed at building up a domestic industrial base. But kick-starting the process of import-substituting industrialization required borrowing heavily from the West in order to buy the capital goods and infrastructure necessary for a diversified industrial base. Servicing these debts in turn required earning foreign exchange and so a continued need to produce for the world market. Latin American countries in particular borrowed large amounts during the 1970s, especially from US banks (Greig, Hulme and Turner 2007: 119), who welcomed this business and were encouraged in extending such credit by the US government, which viewed it as a useful substitute for development aid. During the second half of the 1970s the global economic slowdown also began to affect Latin American countries: as export earnings dropped and thus made it harder to pay off existing loans, they became increasingly dependent on new sources of loans. The Volcker shock made this situation dramatically worse. Much of this debt was in the form of medium-term loans that were renewed regularly, and as debt now suddenly became much more expensive, the debt burden rose quickly, often forcing Latin American countries to borrow more just to maintain the payments on their existing debt. At the same time, the high US interest rates led to capital flight, leading Southern countries to borrow to compensate for this. In this way, many of these countries became caught in a spiral of worsening debt – a situation that became known as the Third World Debt Crisis.

In 1982 the Mexican government announced that it would no longer be able to maintain payments on its debt. And it was clear that several other countries were heading for the same 'solution'. Although Southern demands for wholesale debt cancellation never stood much of a chance, it was also clear that full repayment simply was not possible and that some kind of debt rescheduling was needed. It was in this configuration of circumstances that what would come to be known as 'structural adjustment' emerged. When (most often Southern) countries experienced difficulty meeting their debt obligations, the IMF would step in to offer assistance (both in the form of funds and in the form of assistance in the negotiation of debt rescheduling). Such assistance, however, was conditional on the receiving country committing itself to a wide range of market-oriented reforms, including cuts in government spending, deregulating and opening up markets, the privatization of public enterprises, and the removal of controls on foreign exchange and trade (Greig et al. 2007: 120).

It was in this context that neoliberalism began to assume more coherent organizational forms at the international level and a degree of ideological consistency. The 1970s had been characterized by considerable chaos and confusion, and the economic and financial development of the system had been heavily shaped by pragmatically driven responses to rapidly changing circumstances. During the 1980s, however, the shift

towards more market-oriented policies was increasingly promoted and overseen by a set of organizations that explicitly
embraced principles of austerity and deregulation. Towards
the end of that decade, this configuration would be described
as the 'Washington Consensus', which referred to the ways in
which the IMF, the World Bank and the US Treasury cooper-
ated to spread neoliberal principles and policies around the
globe, as well as their willingness to use financial crises as
leverage to that end. Although one should not overstate the
degree to which these practices were directly informed by
theoretical ideas, what emerged nonetheless was a close affinity between economic policymaking and economic theory's
faith in the virtues of market mechanisms (both in terms of
their ability to deliver efficient allocations and their ability
to promote economic growth and spread wealth) (Serra and
Stiglitz 2008).

There have been numerous critiques of structural adjustment policies (e.g., Stiglitz 2002; Ruccio 2011: ch. 8), with
critics pointing out that they were not about implementing
a neutral and impartial set of economic doctrines but about
imposing policies that reflected and advanced the interests
of Northern capital. These arguments often resembled those
made by dependency theorists in previous decades, when
they had observed the continued dependence of the South on
the North even after the end of formal colonial dependence
(Frank 1978). Whereas the official rationale of structural
adjustment programmes was that they would allow countries
to earn the foreign currency that would enable them to repay
loans, in practice this meant a strong emphasis on exports in
agricultural products and raw materials – a reinforcement of
imperialist patterns of specialization (Veltmeyer, Petras and
Vieux 1997). In other words, the neoliberalization of financial capital provided Northern countries with a particularly
effective way to influence the development of the production
structures of countries in the global South. Once this dynamic
of deregulation was in motion, it became characterized by a
self-reinforcing logic: deregulated capital flows were responsible for the crises that would prompt intervention and so
result in the removal of other barriers to capital mobility,
resulting in turn in a constant pressure to maintain domestic
investment conditions favourable to global capital.

But the pressures of global financial capital were also experienced in Western countries. For instance, when during the early 1980s the French Socialist Party sought to reaffirm its commitment to fiscal activism and deficit spending, the franc came under relentless attack from currency speculators, forcing a major policy turn and the implementation of an austerity programme to appease the global markets. These dynamics resulted in the growing centrality of central banks in the institutional fabric of national states. During the early postwar period, when faith in the benefits and viability of fiscal policy was high, central banks had occupied a decidedly inferior position. But from the 1980s onwards, national central banks emerged as powerful institutions charged with the task of combating inflation and for all intents and purposes serving as domestic enforcers of austerity. The acceleration of European integration can be seen as an attempt to pre-empt the need for a dynamic of continuous downward adjustment. Driven to a significant extent by France after its forced retreat from domestic policy activism, the aim of economic and financial integration was always to 'pool sovereignty' and create an internal market big enough so that Europe could benefit from rather than be constrained by the power of capital (Howarth 2001). But the aim of 'harnessing' the power of finance has always remained an elusive one: German austerity always seemed to have the upper hand over French ambitions for the reconstruction of the social-democratic state at the European level. In many ways European integration has been the pro-active implementation of a particularly severe neoliberalism.

Financial crises

The ways in which increasingly liquid financial markets and increasingly mobile financial capital exerted pressure on national states to converge on a strategy of budgetary austerity and deregulation lent considerable credence to the classic depiction of neoliberalism as the victory of market-led economic development over state intervention. The late 1980s and the early 1990s may have been the high point of such ideas. Fukuyama (1992) famously declared history to have come to an end with the victory of liberal democracy over communism, but such triumphalism was badly shaken by a series of major financial crises at the end of the decade that threw into sharp relief the havoc that financial flows could wreak. Pivotal here was the Asian crisis of 1997, which did much to undermine the idea that following neoliberal strategies offered a viable development model. This was in part due to the sheer severity of the crisis and the way currency speculation plunged an entire region of the world into a prolonged economic recession, but also due to the simple fact that those countries following the IMF rulebook had been affected most severely, whereas those that were quick to impose capital and currency controls in fact remained somewhat shielded from the worst effects of the crisis. Nor was the Asian crisis an isolated incident in this regard: it was preceded by the Mexican crisis of 1994 and followed by the Russian crisis of 1998, both of which involved runs on the currencies of countries that had appeared to have implemented the IMF's advice with considerable diligence.

The role of global finance became a focal point of the emerging anti-globalization movement, which has done a great deal to promote awareness of the dark side of market-led globalization (Buckman 2004). The growing awareness among capitalist elites of the ideological and political challenges to the globalization project served to accelerate a process of reform at the level of global financial governance that had begun after the Asian crisis. Over the past decade and a half, development discourse has assumed a rather friendlier face: it has sought to avoid simple reliance on the stern 'take it or leave it' propositions of structural adjustment, and instead has formulated more inclusive models of globalization. Key features of what came to be known as the New International Financial Architecture included more inclusive summits, representation from developing countries in relevant policy and decision-making processes (e.g., the G7 was transformed into the G20), a greater concern with financial stability (e.g., through the creation of a Financial Stability Forum), and a push for greater transparency (e.g., the promotion of accounting standards) (Soederberg 2004).

But such reforms could not prevent or reverse a serious loss of credibility for the neoliberal paradigm of development and significant damage to the legitimacy and authority of the international financial institutions (Joyce 2012). Many developing countries were now fully aware of the potential consequences of relying too much on IMF/World Bank funding and advice, and in the twenty-first century they increasingly sought to avoid such reliance. Of course this was often easier said than done, as their need to accept the conditionalities of structural adjustment came precisely from the fact that alternative sources of funding (seeking finance in the open market, earning foreign imports or boosting exports) were prohibitively costly and that more autonomous paths of development were out of reach. But especially in Latin America, which during the first decade of the twenty-first century was swept by a 'Pink Tide' that brought to power a series of left-wing governments, the struggle against the rule of global finance assumed concrete organizational dimensions that proved highly consequential. Following its crisis that started in 1998, Argentina in particular, which had long been a reliable neoliberal ally, began to push back against many of the demands made by the IMF, and over the next decade Latin American governments began to cooperate to carve out the space for a regional path of development (Luna and Filgueira 2009). All the same, this has not resulted in a decisive challenge to the power of neoliberal global finance (Yates and Bakker 2014). Tellingly, the Bank of the South, founded in 2009 as an alternative source of financing, has had difficulty becoming fully operational.

Financial instability was by no means limited to the South. At the very end of the 1990s – following the relative stability of Bill Clinton's version of neoliberalism, which had replaced the more uncompromising approach of the Reagan years – the highly symbolic failure of the hedge fund Long-Term Capital Management did much to shake faith in the virtues of deregulated financial markets (Lowenstein 2001; De Goede 2001). LTCM had claimed to have a scientifically unbeatable trading strategy, and its board members included Robert Merton and Myron Scholes (who had only one year before jointly received the Nobel Prize in Economics for their work on the Black-Scholes model for pricing derivatives). And then, at the very start of the new century, the stock market collapsed under the weight of non-performing ICT start-ups. The bursting of the dot-com bubble was especially significant because it had been the key support for the argument that neoliberal reforms had engendered a post-industrial 'new economy' driven by smart technologies and no longer dependent on manufacturing (Lowenstein 2004). All this did a great deal to validate the ways in which critical scholars had understood global finance. One of their key points had always been that, *pace* the claims of orthodox economics, the unshackling and globalization of financial capital resulted not in greater efficiency and growth but essentially constituted an unstable system of casino capitalism, which gave free rein to speculative impulses with little regard for the social and economic foundations of stable growth.

Financialization

And yet, as we discussed at the start of this chapter, this critique of neoliberal finance was always somewhat one-sided. It was becoming clear that, even as this research orientation had a definite salience, it also failed to grasp key aspects of the dynamics of finance – after all, neoliberal finance has evinced a remarkable capacity to pick itself up and keep going, even after a series of major crises (Konings 2011). Many scholars now felt that an exclusive focus on global high finance was in fact rather limiting, especially when it came to explaining the deeper roots of the power and resilience of neoliberal finance. Increasingly the study of global finance in terms of the opposing logic of globalizing financial markets vs. national states was complemented by perspectives that viewed the rise of finance as situated in and produced by specific institutional contexts. Such approaches have converged on the idea that Western economies have in key respects become 'financialized': financial processes have come to occupy a structural centrality in the neoliberal era that they hitherto lacked (Martin 2002). Seen from this angle, the problem is not just the growing influence of global financial markets but rather the ways in which key aspects of the institutional functioning of Western countries are being transformed, from the inside out, on the basis of financial criteria and principles.

When this has been interpreted in a quantitative sense, it entails the claim that a much greater share of profits and GDP now derives from financial circuits than in the past (Krippner 2005; Orhangazi 2008). These approaches have demonstrated in useful ways the growing centrality of finance in the neoliberal economy, but they have tended to formulate their insights through a strongly materialist lens, assessing the role and consequences of financial expansion as a dysfunctional divergence from the more basic and functional forms of financing that facilitated the production of real value in the Fordist manufacturing economy. In this sense, they still take financialization as little more than a symptom of problems in the real economy, and give relatively little attention to the ways in which new financial techniques and devices have reshaped neoliberal economic life at its core, including the very standards that we rely on to measure value. Other scholars have adopted a more qualitative approach, focusing on the specific financial techniques and devices that have shaped neoliberal finance (Froud et al. 2006). Work in the growing field of 'cultural economy' has extended this line of thinking by analysing the ways in which these techniques are not simply the stuff of 'high finance' but have facilitated the penetration of finance into daily life and so driven the growing centrality of financial principles, measures and processes (Martin 2002; Allon 2010). They have begun to write the history of what Langley (2008) has termed 'the everyday life of global finance', tracing the ways in which modern finance involves the 'capitalization of almost everything' (Leyshon and Thrift 2007). Scholars increasingly research finance not simply in terms of the pressures it imposes on states but as a productive force in its own right.

In particular, techniques of 'securitization', which serve to transform illiquid forms of property into tradable assets, have been crucial to the expansionary logic of financial capital. Securitization has a long history, but during the neoliberal era it has been systematically used by financial institutions in order to expand credit. Securitization follows a derivative logic of 'slicing and dicing': disaggregating financial assets and repackaging them to make them tradable. But whereas derivatives have always been seen as emblematic of speculative high finance, securitization has been central to the penetration of debt relations into the daily life of Western societies. It allows financial institutions to originate loans for a fee and then to sell them on the open market (the 'originate and distribute' model). As Davis describes it, 'rather than making loans and holding them on their balance sheet, banks could originate loans and then re-sell them, to be turned into securities and marketed to institutional investors' (2009: 116). This greatly relieved pressure on the balance sheets of financial institutions and thereby reduced the ability of regulations to constrain the expansion of credit. Especially in the UK and the US, securitization techniques have been the basis of the dramatic expansion of household indebtedness since the 1980s (Fuller 2016). Eroding the boundaries that the Glass-Steagall Act of 1933 had erected in the US, banks increasingly restyled themselves as investment banks, rather than limiting their activities to the traditional commercial business of taking deposits and lending.

Much of the demand for securitized assets came from the growth of institutional investors: the combination of dynamic financial markets and dwindling public sources of income provision meant that savings were increasingly channelled into mutual funds and pension funds, which pool a large number of small savings in order to invest them in money and capital markets. Such institutions had an enormous appetite for assets with decent returns, thus providing a continuous force behind the expansion of securitization. Ordinary people were now increasingly integrated into financial markets not just as debtors and savers but also as small investors. As Davis reports, 'the proportion of households invested in the stock market increased from 20% in 1983 to 52% in 2001' (2009: 213). Furthermore, these processes often created some curious feedback loops: in addition to driving the development of securitization, the search for yield was a key source of funds for the new business of hostile takeovers and leveraged buyouts. Whereas in the Fordist era corporations were responsive to a wider variety of parties with an interest in their operation ('stakeholders'), they now increasingly became driven by the imperative of maximizing 'shareholder value'. Corporate restructuring has been a major factor in the growth of unemployment and economic insecurity, so giving a further boost to people's growing dependence on financial markets. In other words, what in mainstream circles has often been welcomed as a democratization of finance was in reality heavily driven by trends of growing inequality and precariousness.

Scholarly interest in the various ways in which households were connected to financial markets increased dramatically in the wake of the dot-com bubble, as financial institutions made a fairly quick recovery, above all by stepping up their securitization strategies. What emerged was the idea of the 'portfolio society', 'in which the investment idiom becomes a dominant way of understanding the individual's place in society. Personality and talent become "human capital", homes, families, and communities become "social capital", and the guiding principles of financial investment spread by analogy far beyond their original application' (Davis 2009: 6). The theory of human capital is one of the most distinctive contributions of neoliberal thought: it refers to the growing tendency to conceptualize capacities, identities and affinities as capital that requires valorization. The neoliberal subject becomes an 'entrepreneur of the self'. Foucault (2008: 219–33) viewed the notion of human capital (e.g., Becker 1964) as one of the most important contributions of neoliberal thought: he saw it as implicitly advancing a critique of the way in which neoclassical economics had reduced labour to a technical factor of production. The notion of human capital brings into view a broader understanding of economic value and growth (Foucault 2008: 232), one that is more attuned to the many opportunities for value capture afforded by the penetration of finance into the fabric of everyday human existence.

The shift towards thinking about everyday finance also had implications for how scholars viewed the global politics of international financial power in the neoliberal era. Nixon's suspension of dollar convertibility was traditionally seen as signalling the inability of the US to sustain its leadership role amid the forces of financial globalization it had set in motion. In subsequent years, such views have been revised in light of the US's continuing ability to attract large capital flows to fund growing deficits and the undeniable influence that Washington wielded in diffusing norms and pressures of liberalized finance across the world (Gowan 1999). But many continued to anticipate the imminent decline of America's financial power in the face of rising contenders (Japan, the European Union and most recently China). In a sense, the US has always been seen as the paragon of neoliberal deregulation and financialization, and hence taken to embody its most fundamental contradiction: the inability of speculative markets to keep themselves going on the basis of an imagined logic of self-referential growth. The shift of focus from high to low finance provided an important new angle from which to examine questions of international financial power. It drew attention to the structural integration of finance in Anglo-American social life and the often surprising sources of value that finance was able to unearth (Seabrooke 2001). From such a perspective, US finance seemed deeply embedded in the fabric of American life. Liquid domestic markets were increasingly seen as a key determinant of a country's ability to wield financial power externally.

Scholars and other commentators, however, have continued to find it difficult to analyse neoliberal finance with the patience and care that it demands, and the financial crisis that began in 2007–8 made this abundantly clear. At the outbreak of the crisis, many were quick to announce the end of neoliberal finance, viewing the event as a decisive demonstration that financial deregulation, speculative markets and growing indebtedness had run their course. But, as deep as the impact of the crisis has been, it has emphatically not signified the end of neoliberalism or a return to the Keynesian welfare state. It is also worth recalling that, for a brief period following the onset of the crisis, Europeans experienced a significant degree of schadenfreude at the sight of an unregulated American capitalism sinking under the weight of its own excessive speculative promises, and thought that this would mean a decisive shift of global power towards Europe's more civilized version of capitalism. But in short order the crisis blew over to Europe, which currently finds itself in a stagnationary dynamic that it is far from clear it will be able to get out of. Far from Europe still being a model that progressives could point to as an alternative to full-fledged US neoliberalism, it has become one of the neoliberal era's main battlefields (Van Apeldoorn 2014; Ryner 2015).

3
Work and Welfare

The effects of neoliberalism on labour are often discussed in terms of its 'recommodification': whereas the institutions of the Keynesian welfare state provided citizens with a certain degree of independence from the pressures of the labour market ('decommodification'), neoliberalism is seen as having once again subordinated human labour to the fiction of being a commodity (to use Polanyian language). This is in many ways a useful framework for understanding what has happened to people's experience of work and labour: much more emphatically than before, one's ability to live – to rent a home, buy decent food, raise a family – is dependent on one's ability to sell one's labour-power to an employer who is willing to buy it. But seen from another perspective, this story suffers from some of the same problems as other attempts to grasp neoliberalism in terms of the rise of 'free markets': it is not sufficiently attuned to the dimension of 'market construction' – which may well operate under the ideological cover of the 'free market' but nonetheless generates results that, on closer inspection, correspond only poorly to that image. It is not simply that the disembedding of labour markets has been conditioned and limited by their institutional context, but also that economic restructuring has been profoundly shaped by political choices and morally charged discourses. In the US this has always been particularly apparent in the way neoliberal welfare reform is allied so explicitly with neoconservative concerns, but we can see similar dynamics elsewhere too, albeit in less spectacular form. Some of the most profound transformations wrought through neoliberalization have been to the ways people work, and the conditions under which this occurs. In this chapter we will explore key aspects of this process.

Changing patterns of work and employment

Even as we emphasize the importance of institutional dynamics in this process, it is appropriate to begin that story by highlighting the centrality of the structural economic decline of the Western manufacturing sector from the late 1960s as a result of intensified inter-capitalist competition within the global economy (Brenner 2006). Whereas in 1960 manufacturing employment as a percentage of total US employment was 31 per cent, a decade later it was 27.3 per cent, and by 1978 it had fallen further to 23.7 (Sachs and Schatz 1994: 5, Table 1). Downward pressure on profitability was the most concrete and readily visible expression of what we now think of as the crisis of Fordism. In this context, the collective power of labour was viewed by many political and economic elites as an obstacle to profitability, a view reinforced by the upsurge in labour militancy from the late 1960s and into the 1970s. The cost and productivity of labour are perennially points of contestation within capitalism, and one important driver of neoliberalism was an attempt, by governments and businesses, to reduce real unit labour costs. An assault on real wage levels and the enhancement of management prerogatives form key parts of the neoliberal transformation of work.

But in the context of the 1970s, the problem from the perspective of company managers and many political elites was still that the collective power of labour prevented significant wage reductions. In earlier chapters we have already examined some of the dynamics that were generated by the interaction of structural economic forces and the growing prominence of neoliberal ideas in that decade. A crucial element of this was the gradual weakening of political commitment to the norm of full employment. The way in which nominal wage rises perversely undid themselves by keeping intact a dynamic of accelerating inflation created a context in which collectivist approaches to regulating wages and work could be framed as continuous political interference with market processes in the name of what Hayek (1976b) disparagingly referred to as 'the mirage of social justice' (the subtitle of the second volume of his *Law, Legislation and Liberty*), causing problems without delivering benefits. Full employment thus came to be viewed as an effect of well-functioning market mechanisms and could not itself be a policy objective.

Here deindustrialization, while in key respects at the origin of the problems, also appeared as a promising source of possible solutions, since it served to structurally weaken the bargaining power of labour. As we have already seen, the Volcker shock was important in accelerating this process. The dramatic increase in interest rates during the early 1980s which followed that policy turn lured large amounts of capital away from industrial investment, thus giving a significant impetus to the process of manufacturing decline. By 1990 the share of manufacturing in total US employment had fallen further to 17.4 per cent (Sachs and Schatz 1994: 5, Table 1), and this trend has continued: by 2009, it was down to 11 per cent (Lawrence and Edwards 2013: 10, Figure 5). The same trend has been visible across other advanced capitalist economies: in the UK, manufacturing employment as a share of total employment shrank from 32 per cent in 1973 to 11 per cent in 2009; in Germany, it declined from 42 per cent in 1973 to 23 per cent in 2009 (Lawrence and Edwards 2013: 10, Figure 5).

Unions always had a strong foothold in the Fordist manufacturing sector, but, outside of the public sector, they were unable to maintain that strength in the more heavily individualized post-Fordist economy. Trade union membership has declined across the Western world, sometimes precipitously. In the advanced capitalist countries union density has, on average, fallen from 34.1 per cent in 1980 to 16.7 per cent in 2014 (OECD 2016b). As Hacker and Pierson argue of the US context, 'The decline of organized labor has greatly diminished pressure on policymakers to sustain or refurbish commitments to social protection made in the middle decades of the last century' (2010: 180). Key reasons for declining union membership density include legislation making recruitment more difficult, a decentralization of industrial bargaining, job losses in areas of union strength, and the geographical relocation of production to areas in which union organizing is more prohibitive. In some cases, trade union power was confronted directly, but generally it was eroded through labour market deregulation in its various forms, as well as through the broader restructuring of corporate production.

Deindustrialization drove a sharp increase in unemployment during the 1980s, and while employment rates did subsequently improve, a central feature of neoliberalism has been a generalized increase in unemployment as compared with the postwar boom decades. Outside of the US, few economies were able to re-establish the low rates of unemployment that prevailed in the 1950s and 1960s. Long-term unemployment, defined as being out of work for twelve months or more, also rose. Across the G7 countries, long-term unemployment as a proportion of total unemployment increased markedly from 2 to 32 per cent between 1970 and 2015. During the same period, the numbers in the US increased from 2 to 18 per cent, with a high of 31 per cent in 2011 (OECD 2016a). Many of those who lost their jobs through industrial restructuring would never find long-term employment again.

Moreover, a high proportion of the new jobs that the neoliberal economy does create are temporary and low-wage. An important development in this respect has been the rise in precarious or 'non-standard' forms of employment such as casual work and short-term contracts, as well as the use of labour hire companies and zero-hour contracts. A recent report from the International Labour Organization (ILO 2015) sums up this trend:

> In advanced economies, the standard employment model is less and less dominant. In emerging and developing economies, there has been some strengthening of employment contracts and relationships but informal employment continues to be common in many countries and, at the bottom of global supply chains, very short-term contracts and irregular hours are becoming more widespread.

Indicative of this trend is that between 1985 and 2007 temporary work increased across the EU economies from 8.3 per cent to 14.7 per cent of total paid employment, and while total employment increased by 26 per cent, temporary work increased by 115 per cent (Herod and Lambert 2016). There are highly gendered and racialized elements to this as well. Across the globe, women are more likely than men to be in precarious forms of work (ILO 2015; ITUC 2011). This has occurred alongside women seeking waged work in greater numbers. Similarly, in Europe migrants are more likely than native-born workers to be in temporary rather than permanent employment (Castles 2015). Here, gendered and racial policies and norms articulate with neoliberal processes of labour market deregulation to drive increases in precarious work.

More generally, processes of labour market deregulation have allowed managers to deploy labour with more flexibility across the working day and week, especially in the low-paid service sector. While some high-paid, knowledge-intensive workers have certainly enjoyed the benefits, 'flexibility' at work, as Ronaldo Munck argues, has often meant 'a reduction in wages ("labour costs flexibility"), a reduction in the number of workers ("numerical flexibility"), and an increase in the number of tasks the remaining workers had to perform ("functional flexibility")' (2002: 78). There has been a shift in modes of employment as well as in the conditions under which people work, including the rising phenomenon of 'consumptive labour' – the use of consumers to perform the tasks of workers, such as scanning one's own items at the supermarket checkout – which is emblematic of flexibilization, behind which lies the managerial effort to reduce costs (Koeber 2011).

The flipside of deindustrialization in the core capitalist economies has been the expansion of manufacturing capacity in developing economies such as China, India and Indonesia. This expansion, coupled with neoliberal processes of 'accumulation by dispossession', has radically transformed the social and economic landscape as vast numbers of people have become newly dependent upon waged work. Under IMF-mandated structural adjustment programmes, or as a consequence of 'free trade agreements' such as NAFTA, millions in the global South have been divorced from their previous means of livelihood through land acquisition or the undercutting of local producers by agribusiness (Ferguson and McNally 2015: 10). Such processes have helped swell the ranks of the global working class to over 3 billion, up from approximately 2 billion in 1980 (Ferguson and McNally 2015: 9). This has led to a mass movement of labour in search of work, including both internal and outbound migrants. Yet, while capital has been substantially freed from many of the constraints imposed during the early postwar period, the same is not true for the majority of workers, whose movement across borders is tightly regulated. Many become 'undocumented workers lacking civil and labour rights...[and constitute] a vulnerable and hyper-precarious section of the working class whose insecurity contributes to the lowering of general levels of real wages' (Ferguson and McNally 2015: 5). Others, meanwhile, work under restrictive temporary employment regulations, are tied to particular employers, lack many of the social rights of citizenship, and are similarly precarious and deportable. Of course, there is considerable unevenness to this, with a relatively wealthy, mostly white minority of skilled professionals and managers generally privileged in terms of cross-border labour movement. Similarly, while EU citizens have the right to travel to other EU countries to look for work, and to remain in their destination country after the work has ceased, those from outside the EU do not enjoy such advantages.

While working conditions across the global South do, of course, vary, the main reason for the huge increase in manufacturing capacity in these countries is the ability of corporations to pay workers lower wages than would be required in developed countries. Alongside this, working conditions are generally poor in so far as they tend not to conform to international labour standards, nor, often, to national labour laws. This leads to long hours as well as unhealthy and unsafe work practices. While Western publics often only become aware of such things through media reports on the phenomenon of 'sweatshops', many workers in the global South are routinely subject to poor conditions, in large and small businesses, and in both formal and informal modes of employment. Indeed, for all the talk of a transition to a post-Fordist, knowledge-based economy, much manufacturing work in the global South actually resembles earlier forms of capitalist production in its routinized physicality and working conditions.

Likewise, the phenomenon of precarious work is much more pronounced in developing than in the core capitalist economies. Davis, for example, estimates there are approximately one billion informal workers globally, concentrated in the global South (2006: 178). In relative terms, in 2015 only 25 per cent of workers globally had a permanent contract. In the global North the figure was as high as 74 per cent, whereas in middle-income economies it was 13.7 per cent and in low-income countries only 5.7 per cent (ILO 2015). This has led some to argue that a new 'precariat' class (Standing 2011) has been constituted globally, displacing the old industrial proletariat. However, it is important not to overstate this trend. 'Standard' forms of employment have not disappeared, and workers engaged on a long-term basis, whether part-time or full-time, remain numerically dominant in the advanced capitalist economies (Doogan 2009). Nonetheless, even in those countries, there is a widespread perception of job insecurity, which is likely due to a combination of persistent unemployment, the reduction of protections at work, and the erosion of welfare support. As Doogan argues:

> When people express a fear of redundancy within the next 12 months they are not necessarily suggesting the *likelihood* of a job loss but its *consequence*. If, as in the United States, the loss of a job also means the loss of health benefits, the consequences can be significant. During a period that has seen the erosion of social protection systems and the rise of workfare, fears of job loss will be enhanced, especially if the associated benefit coverage extends to the family. (2009: 192)

Neoliberalism and the welfare state

Alongside these large-scale changes to the nature and geography of work, neoliberal approaches to welfare gained traction by arguing that existing institutional arrangements tend to prevent the kind of price adjustments that would allow labour markets to operate efficiently and generate employment. It has often been pointed out that neoliberalism operates according to the logic of pre-modern medicine, where 'more bloodletting' was the response to the failure of previous rounds of bloodletting to make any positive difference to the patient's condition. The influence of this logic has been especially apparent in the areas of work and welfare, where, no matter how far expectations of lifelong employment have eroded, and no matter how much uncertainty has been introduced into the life of the average citizen, the problem is consistently framed in terms of the ways in which the reforms of the Keynesian era continue to prevent the kind of efficient adjustments that would permit individuals to sell their labour power at the appropriate price. This kind of argument has a long lineage within the neoliberal intellectual movement. Both Hayek (2006) and Friedman (2002) viewed unions as artificially raising the price of labour, thereby contributing to unemployment or reducing the wages of those outside the unionized sectors. Their solutions to this problem were similar, focusing on ending union privileges (what Friedman called union monopolies and Hayek union coercion), while Friedman (2002: 35) also called for the abolition of minimum wage rates because of their market-distorting effects.

The tenacity of this logic of 'more bloodletting' suggests that it is not simply an intellectual argument rooted in specific economic insights, but also involves a profound moral dimension. The alliance between neoliberal reason and the moral fervour of neoconservatism has been nowhere more evident than in the area of labour market and welfare state reform. This is further confirmed by the fact that neoliberal reformers have always had a high degree of tolerance for the kind of institutional interventions that have served to reinforce the link between income and work, even when those interventions in no way conform to any notion of free market exchange. Indeed, one wonders what Hayek and Friedman would have made of some of the labour market transformations carried out in their name. For example, whereas Republicans in the US have aggressively pursued 'right-to-work' laws, outlawing the compulsory payment of union fees (which had been justified as a way of pricing the positive externalities accruing to non-union members by virtue of the wages and conditions won on their behalf by the union), Friedman opposed such prohibitions, arguing that 'given competition among employers and employees, there should be no reason why employers should not be free to offer any terms they want to their employees', including that they be unionized (2002: 115). Similarly, while many a neoliberal government has restricted the ability of trade unions to take industrial action, Hayek's position was that 'neither the right of voluntary agreement between workers nor even their right to withhold their services in concert is in question' (2006: 235).

Neoliberal intellectuals and think tanks have long characterized the welfare state as a vast, bloated bureaucratic apparatus that serves special interests and creates welfare dependency rather than serving the needy. It is typically viewed as embodying the chief defects of collectivism: a substitution of politically inspired goals for individual freedom; interference with the risk-reward mechanisms of free markets; and good intentions leading to perverse outcomes. Within this broad consensus, however, leading neoliberals differed in their analyses of the problems of the welfare state as well as their preferred solutions. Hayek, for example, saw a role for government in providing 'some minimum of food, shelter and clothing sufficient to preserve health and the capacity for work' and in 'organising a comprehensive system of social insurance' against sickness and accident (1945: 144, 145). But there was great danger, he argued, in the tendency of states to assume the role of mitigating market-based risk altogether, of taking the 'paternalistic' approach and using redistributive mechanisms to ensure that people 'are given what some experts think they need' (2006: 227). Friedman called this latter danger 'equality of outcome', which he considered deeply inimical to capitalist freedom, while the only path consistent with individual liberty is the 'equality of opportunity' provided by markets in which all are free to pursue their chosen ends given their particular resources (Friedman and Friedman 1980: 163–72). He called for a complete dismantling of the welfare state, replacing (in the US context) all current schemes with a negative income tax, whereby those whose incomes fell below a certain threshold would receive payments from the government at a set rate. This would slim the state's self-interested bureaucracy, stem the ever-expanding welfare bill, prevent those not requiring assistance from accessing benefits, and ensure that poor people would end their dependency on welfare.

Neoliberal think tanks took up these themes with considerable enthusiasm and often allied them to conservative arguments about the dangers of the welfare state. At first glance, this alliance might seem strange. Neoliberal and conservative traditions of thought are based upon quite distinct and, in some cases, antithetical intellectual foundations. In particular, whereas neoliberalism is based upon a quite strict methodological individualism, conservatives value the deep underlying institutions that provide structure and order to Western societies – such as the 'traditional family', the military, deference to authority and religion. Conservatives also tended to be anti-rationalist, and therefore sceptical of the ability of human reason to understand society in its complexity. Indicative of these differences, Hayek wrote 'Why I Am Not a Conservative' (the Postscript to *The Constitution of Liberty*), seeking to distinguish his views from those of mid-century conservatives whom he saw as part of the collectivist consensus that was so damaging the foundations of Western civilization (2006: 343–55).

Nonetheless, there are areas of significant intellectual complementarity between neoliberal and conservative thought. Most obviously, both seek to preserve the essential foundations of the capitalist economy and both stand in opposition to any force that would seek to erode those foundations – especially socialist and socialist-influenced ideologies and movements. In Hayek too there are affinities with conservatism: even as he railed against it, his deep scepticism regarding the capacity of human reason to understand the economy in its complexity, which is at the heart of his understanding of the virtues of the price mechanism in a market economy, also resonates with the anti-rationalist disposition of many conservatives (Scruton 2006). There are other more specific intersections between neoliberalism and conservatism that became particularly salient in the context of the 1960s and 1970s. For example, some of Friedman's popular writings evince a conceptual slippage between the individual and the family as the basic unit of analysis, thus implicitly acknowledging the significance of one of the most valued institutions within conservative thought. And social and political forces that strained against the traditional model of the family – the rise of feminism and the decline of the Fordist family wage – were widely seen as causes of the disarray of the 1970s (Cooper 2017). If the individual occupies a central role in neoliberal thought, this notion always remained highly gendered, closely bound up with traditional understandings of a sexual division of labour.

We should not, however, make too much of the mutual consistency of neoliberalism and neoconservatism on a purely intellectual level, but instead emphasize the ways in which they became allied in specific historical circumstances: what ultimately united these potentially contradictory movements was a common enemy in the form of the 'new class'. This was a concept popularized by neoconservative intellectuals such as Irving Kristol and Daniel Bell, referring initially to the radical social movements of the 1960s, whose members, they alleged, having failed to bring about their desired social revolution, found employment within the state, and used their positions of influence to promote their radical ideological visions, including moral permissiveness, equality of outcome, and a basic hostility to capitalism and Western values, while claiming to work in the public interest (Cahill 2001; Ehrenreich 1990). This brought the conservatives into similar conceptual territory to the neoliberals. The public choice wing of the neoliberal thought collective, through theorists such as James Buchanan and Gordon Tullock, had developed a critique of public servants and politicians as motivated by self-interest rather than the public interest, and argued that the state was vulnerable to capture by organized lobby groups, such as public sector or teacher unions. Thus, neoliberals railed against privileged 'special interests', sheltered from competition within the state, and pursuing their particular conception of the good at the expense of economic efficiency.

The critique of 'special interests' and the 'new class' facilitated a certain rapprochement and at times even a fusion of conservative and neoliberal critiques of the welfare state. For conservatives, new-class special interests were responsible for the breakdown of the traditional family, particularly among African Americans. Conservatives such as Lawrence Mead (1986; 1993) and Charles Murray (1984) argued that this

breakdown was the chief cause of poverty and was reproduced by a culture of 'welfare dependence'. Similarly, neoliberals viewed the new class as responsible for fostering a
culture of welfare dependency by creating incentives for the
poor to shelter from market discipline. Indeed, public choice
theory suggested that welfare bureaucrats had an interest in
increasing the number of those dependent upon welfare payments since this constituted their client base and was a chief
measure of their power and prestige within the state. For
both neoliberals and conservatives, devolving the provision
of welfare from the state to the private sector or the family
would serve to break the power of the entrenched new class.
Conservatives saw this as opening up the possibility of faith-
based groups taking a stronger role in administering welfare
(and, indeed, becoming involved in other social services such
as schools) and creating incentives for the maintenance of
traditional family structures (Hackworth 2012). Neoliberals saw it as ensuring that the provision of welfare and
other social services would be allocated according to individual preferences through markets rather than according
to the preferences of self-interested bureaucrats and politicians. Friedman's proposed voucher scheme is another good
example. Friedman argued that a competitive market could
be created for schooling by issuing all parents of school
children with a 'voucher' worth a fixed amount that could
then be used to purchase education, with schools free to set
their own fee levels. The claim was that schools would then
have an incentive to respond to the preferences of parents
(Friedman and Friedman 1980: 193–210). With respect to
workfare (discussed later in this chapter), although some
neoliberals saw it as overly paternalistic, it was generally
viewed favourably as it created incentives for poor people to
look for paid employment.

As we have stressed throughout this book, it is a difficult
task to pinpoint the precise impact of such ideas. As Burgin
perceptively argues:

> the relationship between abstract ideas and processes of politi-
> cal change is challenging to represent. The modes of transmis-
> sion that the Mont Pelerin Society's members employed were
> varied and diffuse, and public manifestations of their policy

ideas always followed processes of mediation and contestation that rendered them irrevocably transformed. (2012: 223)

In the case of the transformation of the welfare state, the neoliberal intellectual movement certainly helped reorient public debate. No doubt it also provided a set of conceptual frameworks that gave coherence to the intuitions of many conservative policymakers. Yet it also resonated with a broader history and discourse of race and gender and was congruent with transformations to work and the labour market that had been in train since the 1970s. Neoliberal politicians such as Ronald Reagan and Margaret Thatcher similarly made attacks upon the welfare state and a supposed 'culture of entitlement' central to their public rhetoric. Reagan's infamous racially charged attacks on 'welfare queens', evoking an image of non-white women leading a luxurious lifestyle that hard-working Americans paid for, were a case in point.

Transformations of welfare

For a long time, scholars took neoliberal rhetoric as an overly literal guide to the practical effects of neoliberalism on the welfare state. However, the welfare state has not been destroyed by neoliberalism – far from it. Indeed, when considered in a quantitative sense, it has actually grown in many parts of the world. Expenditures on welfare and health comprised over 85 per cent of the growth in government expenditure between 1970 and 1997 (Sanz and Velazquez 2007: 917). Alongside this, the tax and transfer systems operated by states mitigated, at least to some extent, the explosion in market-based income inequality (Mahler, Jesuit and Paradowski 2013). Moreover, some universalist welfare institutions, such as Britain's National Health Service, which would ostensibly seem antithetical to neoliberalism, have persisted throughout the neoliberal era. But while it has not been retrenched, the welfare state has been radically changed through neoliberalization. In ways that are not readily apparent from quantitative indicators regarding its size, the welfare state has been extensively marketized and corporatized.

Private providers have increasingly been engaged in the provision of social services, while unemployment assistance or insurance has become increasingly onerous and punitive and is closely linked to ensuring recipients' availability for low-paid and precarious forms of work.

Of course, to some extent welfare has always had a 'central role...in the regulation of marginal labor and the maintenance of civil order' (Piven and Cloward 1971: xvi), and we should not exaggerate the extent to which in earlier times welfare arrangements were external to, or provided an effective escape from, the pressures and imperatives of capitalist competition. Nevertheless, whereas the postwar welfare state, combined with a regime of close to full employment, gave people a certain degree of leeway in relation to the pressures of the labour market, the neoliberal welfare state has become closely attuned to the requirements of corporate profitability and the specific concerns of employers. These phenomena require careful examination in terms of the relationship between neoliberal theory and practice, as well as a sensitivity to the uneven development of neoliberalism and the ways in which it has been overlaid upon existing institutions.

The marketization of social services has been an important trend in neoliberal forms of governance, but there are certainly antecedents of this in earlier eras of capitalist regulation. Equally, however, it is clear that governments have increasingly constructed markets to provide social services as part of the broader neoliberal reconstitution of the state. Since the 1980s, states have introduced or expanded market mechanisms and forms of private delivery in the arenas of education, healthcare, prisons, childcare, unemployment assistance and elderly care (Gingrich 2011). A range of measures have been adopted to this end, including vouchers, tenders and contractual governance as well as the direct or implicit funding by the state of private providers in order to subsidize markets that otherwise would not exist or, if so, would service only a niche population.

There is considerable unevenness in this process, and in many cases the extent of marketization has been shaped by inherited institutional structures. This is evident, for example, with respect to the marketization of childcare in Britain and Sweden. Until the 1990s, childcare in Britain was predominantly provided within the household, with only limited services available through local councils. But by 2011, as a result of the New Labour government introducing marketization to increase the supply of childcare, 72 per cent of children were cared for by for-profit providers, 17 per cent by not-for-profits and 12 per cent directly by the state. Sweden, in contrast, due to its institutionalized principle of universal access to welfare, had a long history of the state directly providing childcare services for children of working parents, as well as more limited services for the children of the unemployed. In 1991, the short-lived centre-right government introduced marketization, yet by 2011 this had not dislodged the state as the main provider, with 81 per cent of children still cared for by state-run childcare centres, 11 per cent by not-for-profits, and only 8 per cent by for-profit providers (Brennan et al. 2012).

Such unevenness notwithstanding, there are some commonalities to the processes of marketization. First, users of marketized services come to be defined as consumers, or customers. This tends to erode the concept of a public sphere in which services are provided by states as a right of citizenship or residence. Second, marketization tends to generate inequalities with respect to access and standards. This is driven by factors such as the level at which the fee (if any) is set to access the service in cases where a user-pays principle operates; the extent to which wealthier people are able to purchase higher quality or a greater variety of services than poorer people; and the availability and quality of services for those who live in remote or regional areas. Third, because many services are labour intensive, efficiency gains are generally achieved through reductions in salary costs – either through lower pay or reduced staffing numbers. This in turn tends to reinforce broader patterns within the labour market of a growing low-waged and precariously employed sector. Fourth, despite marketization often being justified by appeal to the need to increase consumer choice, this is undermined in practice by the high transaction costs involved in changing service providers, such as with respect to childcare centres or schools. Fifth, it is rare for marketization to contain costs for consumers, especially, as is often the case, where providers are able to increase their charges over time. Finally, marketization contributes significantly to what scholars have termed the 're-privatization of social reproduction', which includes processes of 'biological reproduction, reproduction of the labour force [and] reproduction of provisioning and caring needs' (Bakker 2003: 77). Neoliberalism has 're-privatized' social reproduction by making households more dependent on the market for things such as healthcare, education and childcare, or they have been forced to fend for themselves. Indeed, several of the areas of consumption that have grown as a proportion of household expenditures in the US are precisely of this type (Dunn 2009: 235), with a parallel rise in the use of debt to finance such expenditures (Roberts 2013: 30).

The trend towards the marketization of the welfare state is driven in part by the self-imposed fiscal limitations of governments resulting from decades of tax cuts. Yet, as noted earlier, public expenditure on social services has not decreased. Indeed, many forms of marketization are predicated on recurrent subsidies by the state to private sector providers. Nonetheless, in many countries, neoliberalization has entailed the imposition of fiscal austerity on public services such as schools, universities and hospitals. It is in this context that there has been a turn to corporate sponsorship of public services. For example, Education Funding Partners Inc. is a corporation that 'works to match schools with opportunities to receive funding, in exchange for marketing opportunities at the schools on behalf of Fortune 500 corporate sponsors' (Molnar 2013). Indicative of which, in 2013 it brokered a deal between the retail firm Target and 227 schools across the US to include the Target logo on the lists that inform parents of the supplies (pens, bags, notepads, etc.) required for school each year.

This prompts a consideration of the ways in which public services are being commodified as the logic of market valuation becomes more central to welfare provision. Indeed, a massive 'public services' industry has developed that is dependent upon ongoing funds and contracts flowing from the public to the private sector. Some of the biggest providers of social services around the world are now major publicly listed corporations. Serco, for example, is a listed, UK-based corporation providing what were once called public services, which means its main customers are governments. In Britain, for example, it owns or operates prisons, immigration detention centres, railways, speed cameras and school inspections, among other public functions (Harris 2013). While UK-based, its operations are global, with contracts in Europe, North America, the Middle East and the Asia-Pacific. In 2015 its revenues totalled $4.8 billion (Gledhill 2016). Another example is ABC Learning, a for-profit childcare company, which was listed on the Australian stock exchange in the early 2000s. It grew to own 2,323 childcare centres in the US, Australia, New Zealand and the UK, becoming the largest listed company in the world specializing in childcare. Indicative of the reach of financialization into privatized social service provision, it had leveraged its real estate holdings to fund its expansion into the childcare market. Since it had also engaged in margin borrowing, when the global financial crisis hit in 2007–8, 'margin calls' were made on it, leading to the collapse of its share price and the company going into receivership (Brennan 2014).

'Workfare' is another plank of the neoliberal transformation of the welfare state. It refers to a more punitive approach to the provision of unemployment assistance. As Peck puts it, 'The essence of workfarism... involves the imposition of a range of compulsory programs and mandatory requirements for welfare recipients with a view to *enforcing work while residualizing* welfare' (2001: 10). Workfare policies have been symbiotic with the growth of more precarious forms of employment, which, as we have seen, have spread substantially under neoliberalism.

Workfare of course has historical antecedents, such as Britain's nineteenth-century Poor Laws and the way they made the workhouse the *sine qua non* of public assistance. But it was an approach that seemed to have been largely eradicated during the early postwar period. President Nixon was one of the first to use the term 'workfare', in the context of his programme to embed work requirements into the receipt of federally funded welfare (Peck 2001: 90). Reagan also facilitated workfare-type programmes through the 1981 Omnibus Budget Reconciliation Act, which made eligibility for welfare more difficult, lowered payments, 'and offered further inducements for states to develop welfare-to-work programs' (Peck

2001: 91). But it wasn't until the Personal Responsibility and Work Opportunity Reconciliation Act, signed into law in 1996 by Bill Clinton, that workfare became central to the way in which US governments regulated the poor. The Act placed time limits on the receipt of unemployment assistance payments (a maximum of five years over one's lifetime, and no more than two years contiguously). It also required single parents receiving payments to work for at least thirty hours per week, and pushed others into low-paid work. States had significant discretion as to how these principles would be implemented, and in some cases pursued policies that were much harsher than was mandated by federal laws. A combination of the onerous and punitive nature of the new workfare approach and the concurrent economic boom, which led to an increased demand for labour, led to a dramatic fall in the number of welfare claimants. Yet most former welfare recipients were not able to secure full-time work, nor escape poverty (Boushey 2002).

It wasn't only in the US that workfare came to define the regulation of the poorest sections of society. By the early twenty-first century, a workfarist orientation was evident in numerous capitalist states. Even in Europe, where welfare states remained much more socially protective than in the US, workfarist approaches have become increasingly evident. During the 1980s and early 1990s, many European states responded to the generalized increase in unemployment stemming from the crisis of the postwar order by shifting towards labour market 'activation' policies, which means using a range of measures to 'activate' the unemployed to find work. Such policies typically involved assisting the unemployed through access to training and re-skilling so as to better equip them for a rapidly transforming labour market – what is often called the 'human resources' approach to activation, yet workfare gradually came to inflect the regulation of the unemployed. In Britain, for example, the New Labour government built upon the earlier Conservative governments' steps down the workfare road by introducing its 'New Deal' approach to unemployment. This placed new obligations on unemployed people, especially the young, making it compulsory for them to engage in one of four approved 'welfare to work' activities – subsidized private sector employment, work for the voluntary sector, work for an environmental taskforce, or full-time education (Jessop 2003) – and introduced a contractual basis for unemployment assistance by requiring the unemployed to sign a 'Jobseeker's Agreement'. As Jessop notes, it 'is a typical neo-liberal programme and is intended to eliminate welfare dependency' (2003: 13). It is the characteristics of the unemployed, rather than the labour market, that are targeted for modification. Yet, in contrast to the US, New Labour's workfare programmes were introduced alongside a range of other social welfare measures designed to increase access to services and mitigate market-based inequality, including an expansion of funding for childcare, a national minimum wage and family tax credits.

Similarly in Germany it was a centre-left government that rolled out major workfarist transformations to the state. The 'Hartz' reforms (named after Volkswagen's Personnel Director Peter Hartz, who chaired the commission from which the recommendations arose) were enacted by Chancellor Gerhard Schroeder's Social Democrat-Green coalition government. Introduced between 2003 and 2005, they led to an integration of unemployment and social welfare payments, which reduced benefits for many, brought in new sanctions for those who refused offers of work, and, like in Britain, established a more contractual approach to the unemployed (Tompson 2009: 223–36). One can readily see how this has complemented precarious and low-paid forms of work, while the period since the late 1990s in Germany has seen an increase in wage inequality, 'driven by increasing inequality in the bottom half of the distribution' (Fredriksen 2012: 9).

Meanwhile, the concept of 'flexicurity' has become increasingly influential within the EU. To its proponents it offers the 'best of both worlds' – the economic security provided by social-democratic welfare states and the competitiveness facilitated by a more neoliberal approach to flexible labour markets. At the heart of flexicurity approaches is a focus on active labour market programmes (ALMPs) designed to provide workers with sufficient 'lifelong learning' to quickly transition between different types of waged work. Flexicurity takes its inspiration from the schemes pioneered by the governments of Denmark and the Netherlands in the 1990s. While such countries, with their relatively generous welfare states, strong trade unions and history of coordinated approaches to economic regulation, have remained much more socially protective than countries such as the US and Britain, within Europe as a whole 'a tendency towards weakening social protection for the unemployed and the spread of ALMPs with a workfare complexion has nevertheless been apparent across all regime types' (Heyes 2013: 74). This illustrates not only the variegation and unevenness of 'actually existing neoliberalism' (Brenner and Theodore 2002; Peck and Tickell 2002), but also how neoliberal transformations are mediated and inflected by pre-existing local institutions.

Neoliberal welfare has proceeded somewhat differently in many developing countries, including Bangladesh, Cambodia, Turkey, Chile, Mexico and Brazil, where conditional cash transfers (CCTs) have emerged as the chief form of state-provided welfare. CCTs entail cash payments to poor households on the condition that they conform to specified behaviours, such as sending children to school, complying with child vaccination schedules, and the use of primary health services. Unlike workfare programmes, which at the extreme force recipients into low-paid precarious work and make welfare receipt more onerous, CCTs typically take the form of poverty reduction programmes and focus heavily on building the 'social capital' of the next generation of workers. Yet there is more than a passing similarity between such programmes and the workfarist trend in the global North (Peck and Theodore 2010), in so far as both aim to modify the behaviour of recipient groups. In the case of workfare programmes, the goal is to end the supposed behaviour of welfare dependency in order to foster greater self-reliance. CCTs also seek to make households more self-reliant, especially by taking responsibility for investing in their children as human capital. Both approaches are also premised upon the need to adjust people to the effects of broader neoliberal restructuring, whether this be the rise of more precarious and low-waged labour markets, or the greater exposure of the economy to transnational capital and market imperatives. It is perhaps little wonder then that CCTs have been viewed favourably by the World Bank (Fiszbein et al. 2009).

There are often highly gendered and racialized elements to workfare programmes. One of the most significant economic and social developments that has overlapped with the neo-liberal transformation of states has been the large increase in female labour force participation. This is a global phenomenon in part driven by factors quite separate to neoliberalism, especially the rise of the feminist movement and its demands for equal opportunity, as well as the provision of equal pay, maternity leave and childcare to facilitate women's return to paid work. Yet it is also a response to the need to boost household income in the face of declining or stagnant real wages. Notwithstanding moves towards gender equality in several areas, in many countries the neoliberalization of welfare has entailed a more punitive approach towards women, particularly poor single mothers, 'removing [their] option to remain at home with their children, and propelling them into the low-wage labour market' (Collins and Mayer 2010: 107). In the US, workfare has combined with a history of institutionalized racism, deindustrialization and federalist fiscal austerity, especially in inner cities, to create new racialized inequalities and new regimes for regulating minority groups such as the African-American population. Indeed, much of the discourse surrounding the rise of workfare policies implicitly or explicitly relied on images of dysfunctional, irresponsible and welfare-dependent African-American families (Soss, Fording and Schram 2011: 63). Even the name of Clinton's headline workfare bill, focused on 'Personal Responsibility', was part of this racial and gender-coded discourse. As Abramowitz argues, advocates of workfare

> built public support for cutting the rolls by playing to gender and racial stereotypes and demonizing big government... They stigmatized single mothers for failing to comply with prescribed wife and mother roles; depicted women of color as matriarchal, hypersexed, and promiscuous, and blamed single mothers for most of society's woes. (2006: 337)

Whether by intention or otherwise, workfare became symbiotic with some of the broader economic transformations of the neoliberal era. It provided institutional support to the structures and arrangements upon which corporate profitability in many industries came to depend. Neoliberal approaches to welfare have gradually converged on a logic that focuses on the attributes of the unemployed individual, rather than on the elements of an economic system that often fails to provide sufficient opportunities for waged work (Peck and Theodore 2000). It is thus consistent with the broader shift in macroeconomic policy towards inflation targeting and a tolerance of higher rates of unemployment compared to the postwar boom years. This in turn has helped to keep labour costs in check, since unemployment exerts downward pressure on wages.

As we have seen, by making unemployment payments far less generous and qualifying for them much more onerous, neoliberal approaches to welfare encouraged the expansion of precarious, low-paid forms of work. The growth of such forms of work provided another avenue through which businesses were able to reduce costs and increase flexibility in the wake of the 1970s economic crisis. As critics of Reagan's cuts to welfare funding noted at the time, 'income-maintenance programs are coming under assault because they limit profits by enlarging the bargaining power of workers with employers', and 'if the desperation of the unemployed is moderated by the availability of various benefits, they will be less eager to take any job on any terms' (Piven and Cloward 1985: 13, 26).

Furthermore, as a way of managing the social dislocation and dissent engendered by the neoliberal restructuring of welfare and of the state more generally, states have increased their coercive surveillance and disciplining of the poor. As Wacquant has argued, in the US and elsewhere this has entailed the rise of a 'prisonfare' approach under which increasing rates of incarceration have been used to regulate those dispossessed through neoliberalization: 'economic deregulation required and begat social welfare retrenchment, and the gradual makeover of welfare into workfare, in turn, called for and fed the expansion of the penal approach' (2009: 58).

4
Corporate Power

Prior to the US-led invasion of Iraq in 2003, it is unlikely that many would have heard of a corporation called Blackwater – the private military company that provided armed security personnel to the US military. The firm achieved global notoriety in 2007 after it was revealed that Blackwater security guards had killed seventeen unarmed Iraqi civilians in Nisour Square, Baghdad. Although the private security forces contracted by the US government had been granted certain legal immunities, four contractors were eventually brought to trial in 2014, with three found guilty of manslaughter and one of murder. The Nisour massacre focused public attention on the outsourcing of the US military. While private mercenaries had been part of warfare for centuries, 'in the wake of globalization and the end of the Cold War, the private military market has expanded in a way not seen since the 1700s' (Singer 2003: 40). Indeed, private contractors had become central to the prosecution of the US government's 'War on Terror'. There are many reasons for this, but among them are the convenience it affords the state in being able to shield its military operations, including casualties, from public scrutiny through contractual confidentiality.

From a classic liberal point of view, this is a remarkable development, as its notion of political organization is centrally guided by the separation of public authority – and in particular the use of physical force – from the economic sphere. The role of Blackwater during the Iraq War therefore prompts consideration of some of the processes and implications of the transformation of corporations through neoliberalism, and the new ways in which they have been brought into relations with states. The corporation is a pervasive feature of modern economic life. As such, it is one of the main institutions through which most people encounter the concrete effects and modalities of neoliberalism – whether it be through work, consumption or as they deal with the more indirect but no less crucial aspects of corporate production such as pollution, political influence or advertising. Furthermore, many of the changes to state regulations and functions described in Chapter 1 revolve around the role of corporations.

This chapter begins by looking at the ways corporations have changed as a result of neoliberal state transformations, especially privatization and deregulation. We also consider how the rise of financialization, spurred on by waves of deregulation, has brought new dynamics to the conduct of corporations and facilitated the increasing transnationalization of capital. The chapter then examines how neoliberal theorists have sought to understand the corporation, and identifies the crucial role played by corporate funding in enabling the neoliberal intellectual movement to expand from a small group of intellectuals into a network of institutions with multimillion-dollar budgets. Finally, we examine the transformations of corporate power as a result of neoliberal restructuring.

Corporate transformations

Neoliberal transformations to states have facilitated an expansion in the scope of corporate activity. This is due in large part to privatization, which involves the creation of privately owned, for-profit corporations through the sale of activities previously controlled by the public sector. An indication of the extent of this transformation is the following from Glyn: 'The share of state-owned enterprises in global GDP is estimated as falling from more than 10% in 1979 to less than

6% in 2004...Privatized firms represent around 30% of the market capitalization of stock markets outside the USA' (2006: 37). But other, related policies like deregulation have also played an important role in facilitating the growing reach of corporate activity, as it is typically designed to remove restrictions on the activities of corporations – enabling them, for example, to deploy labour more flexibly throughout the working day and week, or to move into markets from which they were previously barred. Deregulation allows private sector competitors into once state-monopolized industries, and new corporations have been formed to profit in this space. Where once a single state-owned entity provided services such as electricity, gas and telecommunications, in many countries the service is now largely provided by private corporations.

But it is not simply the case that the leeway of private corporations vis-à-vis the public sector and regulation has been increased greatly; corporations have also been brought into the internal operations of states and become involved in public programmes once organized directly by states themselves. Such processes have created enormous opportunities for corporations to profit from the public provision of services, infrastructure and advice. This means that estimates of the extent of privatization, telling as they are, in fact greatly underestimate the role of corporations in contemporary capitalism. They leave out, for example, public-private partnerships, the contracting out of routine tasks (such as cleaning and security), the engagement of private providers by the state to produce or run new facilities or services, and the use of private contractors to work alongside public employees who are performing the same role (such as in the military). All of these phenomena are by now entirely mainstream in most Western countries.

Furthermore, even those areas of the state's operation that in principle remain fully in public control and democratically accountable are increasingly adopting corporate techniques and methods. As Eagleton-Pierce notes, there has been an 'extraordinary emphasis on management during the neoliberal period' (2016: 177), and the growing influence of techniques associated with the 'new public management' has meant that states, in their core governmental operations, work more and more like corporations. Typically this entails disaggregating government departments and agencies into cost centres, subject to budget constraints, with measurable and pecuniary-based performance targets used to 'incentivize' public servants in place of a less quantifiable public service ethos. In many cases, public sector agencies are exposed to competition, such as by having to tender for services they once provided as a matter of course. Internal restructuring of public sector jobs and techniques of private sector management such as performance audits have become much more common (Leicht et al. 2009: 585; Dardot and Laval 2013: 217–31).

Accompanying these changing relations between corporations and public authority has been a more general shift in the ethos and norms of corporate governance. Central here has been the role of financial markets. One significant consequence of neoliberal financial expansion has been the rapid growth of institutional investors such as pension funds and mutual funds, who are often not content to simply 'park' their cash in safe, low-yield assets but are generally on the lookout for more profitable ways to invest their funds. This has been a key driving force behind the rise of the activist investor, who does not simply passively hold corporate stock but will become more actively involved in the governance of the corporations whose stock they buy, intervening to enforce major changes when they feel that a corporation is underperforming. This new approach took a particularly pronounced form in the aggressive strategies pursued by 'corporate raiders' such as private equity funds, whose main purpose was to buy up enough stock to take control of corporations, restructure them, and bring them back to market at much higher prices. The practical upshot of this is that corporate management must ensure that the price of their company's stock remains high – if they fail to do so, they render themselves vulnerable to hostile takeovers. All this has meant a significant shift in the social logic and position of the corporation, with its overriding obligation increasingly being to maximize the return to shareholders (see Davis 2009). A parallel change has been for managers to have larger quantities of their remuneration paid in or linked to shares in the company, which has in turn been a major driver of inequality, creating a class of 'millionaire wage-earners' whose earnings are often several hundred times that of the average employee.

The neoliberal era has also seen the acceleration of processes of corporate transnationalization. While there is a danger in overstating the magnitude of this trend, some important developments are nonetheless evident and worth highlighting. One indication of the growth of transnational corporations (TNCs) has been the increase in absolute numbers, from 35,000 in 1990 to 65,000 in 2000 (Roach 2005: 24), rising further to 79,000 in 2007 (Wilkes 2013: 47). Even more significant, however, has been the growth of TNCs against other economic indicators. For example, while global GDP grew by 173 per cent from 1983 to 2001, 'the value of capital assets owned by the world's largest corporations increased by an astonishing 686 percent during this time' (Roach 2005: 28). Changes in foreign direct investment (FDI) also provide an indicator as FDI measures changes in investment by an entity outside of its home country. Here, there was a major transformation. In the period 1982–2001 FDI outflows grew by 2,100 per cent, as compared with exports growth of 257 per cent and output growth of 195 per cent. This growth in FDI resembled much more the decades of the early twentieth century than the postwar years during which FDI was dampened (Dunn 2009: 160–1). While much of this FDI has actually been concentrated in the core capitalist countries, as will be discussed in more detail in Chapter 5, where it has penetrated low-income economies it has often subverted the import-substitution model of independent development and reshaped those economies in accordance with the accumulation strategies of Western capital.

Alongside the new global corporate geography there has arisen a new set of neoliberal regulations governing trade. Among the most noteworthy are the legion of 'free trade' agreements, such as NAFTA, struck between nation-states, and the principles embodied in the World Trade Organization. Critics of these agreements are right to note a persistent bias towards transnational and large corporations more generally. Indeed, such agreements are often concerned predominantly with introducing ways to protect the rights of investors rather than with free trade per se, such as the codification of monopoly privileges through pharmaceutical patents, or

'Investor State Dispute Resolution' clauses which allow corporations to bring legal action against states for failing to adhere to neoliberal principles. Similarly, the many 'export processing' or 'free trade' zones throughout the world have created geographically specific pockets of territory in which corporations are quarantined from some of the social regulations applying elsewhere in the national jurisdiction. Typically, corporations within these zones benefit from tax and tariff concessions and restrictions on the ability of workers to organize through trade unions. These zones are effectively legally excised from the rest of the country, which has led Aihwa Ong (2006) to describe them as 'spaces of exception'. Special export zones have gained momentum in the late neoliberal period, indicative of which is the Indian government's approval of 700 new zones between 2005 and 2010 (Cross 2010: 357).

Corporations, markets and neoliberal ideology

And yet, despite all this, corporations have at times somewhat faded from view in the academic literature of neoliberalism. If across the global economy many sectors are now dominated by a small number of large corporations, this is hardly what one would expect of a system often referred to as being characterized by 'free markets'. Indeed, at times the prevalence of oligopolies has been taken as evidence for the relatively limited reach of neoliberalism and its rhetoric of free markets and competition.

Such arguments are useful in so far as they alert us to the problems inherent in the common description of neoliberalism as a 'market-based' or 'market-led' system. As we have already seen, there are certainly good reasons to be wary of the claim that neoliberalism is simply about the rule of markets. For one thing, states have often found it necessary to develop a host of new rules and regulatory institutions to enable the entry of new private providers into industries previously dominated by the state and/or to regulate the activities of newly privatized entities, including the protection of consumer rights.

Just as often, however, states have been key actors in support of and regulating monopolistic or oligopolistic positions for corporations. In many cases, even though the contracting out of state services has been widespread, the extent of the markets created in many of these cases is actually quite limited. For example, the contracting out of many public services typically only creates a short-lived market for the contract itself: governments issue a tender (such as the provision of job-matching assistance to the unemployed), corporations will then put in bids, and a contract will be awarded without competition any longer serving as an effective constraint or incentive. Whereas we might have an image of such processes creating a market for public services in which the bulk of citizens become customers of private providers, in many cases what actually occurs is that the government becomes the client and the broader public become users of the service (see Crouch 2011). Similarly, in many cases governments often act to mitigate the risks involved in the provision of important services by corporations (indeed, one of the chief reasons that states came to provide essential public services in the first place was the fear that if left solely to private interests they would not be provided either at the appropriate standard or sufficiently widely). This then becomes a reason why public service contracts drawn up by governments for private corporations are often long-term, further undercutting competition and undermining the ability of price to act as a signalling device. It is also why a range of methods are often used to direct people towards the privately provided service – after all, a captive clientele is one of the major reasons why such ventures are attractive to profit-driven corporations in the first place. Examples include limiting the ability of motorists to evade privately operated toll roads, or limiting the ability of the unemployed to choose their privately operated welfare provider. In each case, provision of public services by corporations bears little resemblance to the abstract market of orthodox economic theory.

Moreover, privatization and deregulation often give rise to a thick layer of private regulation: that is, corporate self-regulation. In many industries, governments allow corporations to regulate their own conduct within a broader framework of publicly established rules. Non-state rule-making is not an exclusively neoliberal phenomenon. As Barkan (2013) reminds us, to some extent the corporation has always been a regulatory institution: historically, it makes more sense to think of the corporation as an institution given a specific mandate of governance with associated privileges than as a 'private' association. But classic liberalism introduced into discourses of public governance precisely the idea of the corporation as a private entity, separate from the exercise of public authority. This was of course challenged during the postwar period, when many Western European countries supported 'corporatist arrangements' with trade unions and large corporations or employer groups to regulate employment conditions and strategic directions within major industries (see Fuchs 2007). But in the rationality of postwar governance such arrangements were only acceptable in so far as they could claim to help construct and implement an impartial general interest. By putting powerful private interests in charge of the formulation and implementation of key areas of public rule-making, neoliberalism departs from both of these rationalities.

Similarly, although neoliberal processes of trade and financial deregulation provided an important impetus for the growth of transnational corporations, this has not in fact brought the world closer to a free market. While about one-third of global trade in 2007 came from transnational corporations, much of this was comprised of intra-firm trade (Wilkes 2013: 48). As Mikler notes, 'Already by the 1990s, as much as 60 to 70% of trade in manufactured goods between OECD countries was intra-firm' (2013: 5). This means a large proportion of international trade entails the transfer of value within a corporation and its affiliates and is thus 'insulated from market forces' (Wilkes 2013: 48). The tendency towards oligopolization – whereby 'all the world's major industrialised sectors are now controlled by five multinational corporations (MNCs) at most, while 28% have one corporation that accounts for more than 40% of global sales' (Mikler 2013: 4) – reinforces this trend. So too does the tendency of large corporations to use contractual arrangements to control their suppliers and customers, and thus transcend markets temporally throughout their supply chain (Wilkes 2013: 50).

But all this can be understood as a limitation of neoliberalism or a refutation of its salience *only* if we work with a very literal understanding of the relationship between neoliberal ideas and practices and turn a blind eye to their ideological dimension. Indeed, the problem here is hardly one that has escaped neoliberal thought – it has in fact been a focal point of debates, and the development of the discourse of the neoliberal intellectual movement has involved a profound shift in the understanding of corporate power and monopolies. In the formative years of the neoliberal movement, there was a broad consensus that corporate monopolies were inimical to economic freedom. At the inaugural Mont Pelerin Society meeting in 1947, for example, key figures from the German ordoliberal movement and the Chicago School advocated a positive role for the state in limiting corporate power and breaking up monopolies. Their vision was of a competitive market-based order, underpinned by a legal and regulative framework provided by the state. During the 1950s, however, neoliberals associated with the Chicago School undertook a rethink of this position and 'began to advocate the idea that monopoly, in all its forms, was almost always undone by the forces of competition; and consequently that a relatively sanguine attitude should be adopted toward both monopoly and large corporations' (Van Horn 2009: 207–8).

Crucial to this intellectual transformation were the Free Market Project and the Antitrust Project, two research programmes that ran from 1946 to 1952 and 1953 to 1957 respectively (Van Horn 2009). Each was housed within the University of Chicago, funded by the Volker Fund and facilitated, in the first instance, by Hayek. The conclusion they reached was that monopoly was less a threat to a free market order than had traditionally been thought by classical liberals. Competition, they came to argue, actually undermined corporate monopolies, and government-owned or regulated monopolies were the real threat to freedom. Moreover, they concluded that government efforts to curb and break up monopolies were actually misplaced. Contrary to popular wisdom, they argued that there had in fact been no identifiable increase in monopolies within the US economy during the twentieth century. They also claimed that the case for breaking up monopolies – anti-trust law – was based on faulty economic reasoning. Rather than focusing on the reduced consumer choice that might result from corporate monopolies or oligopolies, the proper focus, they argued, should be on consumer welfare (see Crouch 2011; Davies 2014; Birch 2015). The economies of scale made possible through corporate concentration often enabled efficiencies that simply weren't available to smaller corporations, and therefore they should not be blocked through anti-trust regulations. Such views were promoted by legal scholars such as Richard Posner and Robert Bork, who were appointed by Ronald Reagan as judges to the Court of Appeals for the Seventh Circuit, and the Supreme Court, respectively.

The corporate funding of neoliberalism

Corporations have themselves been central to the development and dissemination of neoliberal ideas, primarily through their funding of think tanks and related initiatives. Such funding from corporations, their senior managers and large shareholders was crucial to the ability of early think tanks and other centres of neoliberal intellectual activity to sustain themselves during the decades immediately after the Second World War, when their ideas were marginal to the dominant consensus. Indeed, the explosion of neoliberal think tanks from the 1970s would not have been possible without generous corporate donations. Phillips-Fein's comment with respect to the US context, that such support provided 'the material basis for the postwar right' (2009: 297), is also applicable to the neoliberal movement more generally. Perhaps unsurprisingly, neoliberal think tanks have fairly consistently promoted an agenda that advocates freeing corporations from the regulatory constraints of the postwar era and the political marginalization of social interests seen to stand in the way of such a process. This is not to say that the think tanks were made to fall in line with a corporate agenda, merely that corporations would have been unlikely to consistently fund such radical thinking had it not coincided with their perceived interests.

The broad agenda of the think tanks was to reframe public debate so that neoliberal ideas came to be seen as legitimate by the public and policymakers. In the words of Alfred Sherman, Director of the Centre for Policy Studies (a neoliberal think tank established within the British Conservative Party), their role was 'to act as "outsider", "Skirmisher", "trailblazer"...to question the unquestioned, think the unthinkable' (quoted in Cockett 1994: 238). The goal was to articulate a radical alternative to the 'collectivist' consensus and push public debate to the right, especially on economic issues, thus creating a new radicalized centre. Rather than produce original research, the think tanks primarily mobilized the work of key neoliberal intellectuals and made it legible to policymakers or used it to frame current policy issues. As Christopher De Muth (2007), former head of the American Enterprise Institute, notes: 'It is a great advantage when working on practical problems, not to be constantly doubling back to first principles. We know our principles and concentrate on the specifics of the problem at hand.' This often entails condensing and presenting such ideas in a readily digestible format for policy elites. Indicative of this is what Ed Feulner, former head of the Washington-based Heritage Foundation, described as 'the briefcase test', which the Foundation applied to its own publications. As Feulner argues, neoliberal think tanks 'help to translate the works of academics into background papers, issues briefs, monographs, journal articles, congressional testimony and conference topics', and this output 'should be as brief as possible...we try to limit our Backgrounders to ten pages – a document which stands a much greater chance of being put into the briefcase and read *before* the debate than a book which generally ends up on the bookshelf' (1985: 24).

In many public policy debates, neoliberal think tanks have acted as proxies for major corporations, intervening in public and elite discourses to press conceptual frames that legitimate corporate interests and undermine their opponents. A striking example is the way think tanks mobilized in the wake of Hurricane Katrina, which devastated New Orleans in 2005. As Peck argues, neoliberal think tanks quickly used the mass media and their own in-house publications to outline what a proper government response should be. Acting as 'ideological first-responders', they attempted to frame the disaster as an opportunity for corporate-led reconstruction, 'enlarging the role for private enterprise, in market-led development, governmental outsourcing, and urban governance' (Peck 2010: 153).

Another clear case where discursive mobilizations by think tanks have aided corporate interests is climate change policy. The recognition that capitalist forms of production and the sheer scale of present-day economic activity destroy the natural environment, and that public regulation is required to address this, has been a long-standing target of neoliberal think tanks. As Beder notes, 'think-tanks have sought to cast doubt on the seriousness of environmental problems, to oppose environmental regulations, and to promote free-market remedies to those problems – such as privatization, deregulation and the expanded use of private property rights' (2000: 91). They have also engaged in a sustained campaign to undermine the legitimacy of environmental groups, movements and activists, frequently accusing them of harbouring anti-Christian and anti-Western values (Beder 2000: 97). All of this maps neatly onto the interests of many large corporations, which are among the largest environmental polluters and have the most to lose from environmental regulations that impose on them new costs, restrictions and obligations.

One line of argument employed in the anti-environment case is that, even if climate change is a real phenomenon, it is not to be feared as it will present new economic opportunities. Over time, however, the tactics of neoliberal think tanks have shifted from the positive advocacy of novel 'free market' solutions – most notably the creation of a system of 'carbon trading', which is essentially a market for pollution permits – to a sustained campaign designed to cast doubt on the very notion that human economic activity has led or could lead to a rise in atmospheric temperatures. One of the chief tactics has been to cast doubt upon the scientific evidence for climate change, generally arguing either that those scientists who claim that human-induced global warming is a reality are motivated by ideology or personal gain, or that there is no scientific consensus regarding global warming, as exemplified by a recent Heartland Institute publication:

The most important fact about climate science, often over-looked, is that scientists disagree about the environmental impacts of the combustion of fossil fuels on the global climate. There is no survey or study showing 'consensus' on the most important scientific issues, despite frequent claims by advocates to the contrary. (Idso, Carter and Singer 2015)

This campaign seems to have had some success in muddying the waters of public debate on the issue and there has been a shift in public opinion in several countries. It is one of the clearest examples of the relevance of 'agnotology': 'The focused study of the intentional manufacture of doubt and uncertainty in the general populace for specific political motives' (Mirowski 2013: 226).

Neoliberalism and corporate power

The phenomena outlined so far in this chapter sit rather uncomfortably with Milton Friedman's defence of free market capitalism, which rests centrally on the notion that by fostering economic freedom it also promotes political freedom. Concentrations of economic power, he argued, lead to concentrations of political power, whereas free markets will ensure that both economic and political power are dispersed (Friedman 2002). As we have seen, however, neoliberal restructuring has not resulted in a decentralization of economic power: rather, large corporations have increasingly come to inhabit spaces once dominated by governments and states. Neoliberalism has facilitated an increase in the power of large corporations to shape state policy and to pursue their interests politically, and this has led to a significant weakening of democratic influence in key areas of life. To be sure, we should not imagine, as is quite common, the era prior to neoliberalism as a golden age of democracy or social justice – such a view would be utopian in the extreme. But if business has always enjoyed a privileged position within the policy process of capitalist states, neoliberalism has *both* enhanced the structural power enjoyed by large corporations with respect to state policy *and* opened up more areas of policy to direct corporate influence.

This logic is perhaps most readily apparent in the afore-mentioned rise of transnational corporations. Campaigners against corporate power often point to the fact that the market capitalization of the largest TNCs is greater in value than the GDP of most national economies. As a recent *Global Justice Now* campaign points out, 'of the 100 wealthiest economic entities in the world, 69 are now corporations and only 31 countries' (Dodwell 2016). While such comparisons do capture the sheer size of transnational corporations, as well as their capacity to mobilize resources that are simply unavailable to many developing nation-states, they miss other factors contributing to the particular forms of power enjoyed by TNCs. The mobility afforded through operating simulta-neously in different jurisdictions allows them, at least to some extent, to evade some regulations and obligations because 'it detaches the corporation from the exclusive jurisdiction of any one nation-state' (Wilkes 2013: 45). At the global level, regulations governing the conduct of corporations are very weak (Wilkes 2013: 45), giving TNCs freedoms not enjoyed by those companies that are wholly bound to a single national jurisdiction.

Similar logics are at work in the world of finance, which is – notions of the fluidity of finance notwithstanding – pro-foundly shaped by powerful corporations. Of course, it is the speed with which large amounts of finance can now be moved across the globe that has brought new disciplines to bear on state policies. But this logic is shaped not simply by anonymous market imperatives but by the judgements and decisions of key financial institutions such as rating agen-cies, investment funds and banks. Firms such as Moody's and Standard and Poor's rate the credit worthiness not only of corporations and financial assets, but also of states. Their pronouncements affect the ability of governments to take on debt, as a credit-rating downgrade creates the perception that funding a state's debt is a riskier prospect. This has led governments in general to be wary of policy settings that create large and sustained budget deficits. Throughout the neoliberal era this has entailed a fetishization of balanced-budget surpluses as a goal of economic policy and a resolute rejection of the idea that budgetary settings should be viewed as part of a wider set of economic forces and policy goals.

But perhaps the single most telling example of the structural power of finance accreted to large corporations is the state bailout of large banks after the onset of the global economic crisis in 2007–8. States, having allowed such banks to massively expand their operations and trade in new forms of financial instruments, including the securitization of household mortgages, found themselves confronting a situation where these banks had become 'too big to fail' – that is, if they had been left to their own devices, the resulting domino effect of bankruptcies could well have had such devastating economic consequences as to risk a repeat of the economic catastrophe that beset the advanced capitalist economies in the 1930s.

The way in which structural forms of power blend with direct forms of influence becomes fully manifest in the logic of corporate self-regulation, which allows corporations to design the rules that govern their own conduct and against which they will be assessed. While it is often the case that bureaucrats, politicians or state agencies will also play a role in this process, it is nonetheless a clear and widespread instance of neoliberal processes enabling large corporations to directly shape the public policies by which they are regulated. One notable example is the global food industry, which in many countries has established its own codes of practice to regulate food labelling and advertising. Firms view such self-regulation as a way of preventing the imposition of more restrictive government regulations in response to concerns about the effects of processed food on public health. It is therefore perhaps unsurprising that a recent review of the global scholarly literature regarding this phenomenon found that 'commitments in industry self-regulation schemes tend to be relatively vague and permissive', and that most studies 'generally stress the ineffectiveness of existing self-regulation schemes' (Ronit and Jensen 2014: 758).

Processes of privatization have done little to effect a clearer separation of public and private but have primarily served to bring corporations and their representatives directly into the policymaking apparatuses of the state. On the one hand, the retrenchment of public sector employees in key areas has led states to contract out policy advice and design to private sector corporations. On the other hand, various forms of contracting out have necessitated close and ongoing relationships between senior public servants, politicians and corporations as adjustments to contracts or to planned activities are made cooperatively, effectively allowing corporations to shape the course of public policy (Crouch 2011: 86–90). As Wilkes writes, 'the corporate sector...has metamorphosed from making demands on government bodies to actually making policy in areas such as energy policy and social policy' (2013: 145).

Further strengthening the hand of business politically has been the decline in power of the potential countervailing force of organized labour, particularly in the advanced capitalist countries. Several authors (e.g., Hacker and Pierson 2010; Krugman 2009) note the correlation between increasing inequality in the distribution of economic resources favourable to owners of capital and the decline in trade union power and density. Moreover, as such authors also point out, this occurred at a time when corporate political activism and organization increased as a response to the profit squeeze of the 1970s and the surge in trade union and radical social movements demanding greater obligations from business. By the time the global financial crisis began in 2007, several decades of neoliberalization had strengthened the political power of corporations, their owners and their managers. Moreover, corporations had become dependent on the maintenance of neoliberal forms of regulation and service provision. Crouch is therefore surely correct to argue that 'political and economic elites will do everything they can to maintain neoliberalism...They have benefited so much from the inequalities of wealth and power that the system has produced' (2011: 118–19).

5
Power, Inequality and Democracy

On 17 September 2011, up to 2,000 activists marched to Zuccotti Park, near Wall Street, in New York. The context was the ongoing economic and social devastation wrought since the collapse of the sub-prime mortgage market in the US by 2007 and the way it spread through the global economy. The protestors' targets were the major banks and other financial institutions whose offices dominate the skyline in Lower Manhattan. It was their relentless pursuit of profit, protestors felt, that had plunged the economy into crisis through reckless lending practices and speculation in opaque financial instruments. Despite this, neither the banks nor the people running them had been brought to account by governments – instead, they had been bailed out with public funds and were returning to their former practices while distributing the proceeds as bonuses.

'We are the 99%' quickly became the most identifiable motif of the protest, and was adopted by many of the other similar occupations and protests that rapidly sprang up across the world. The slogan expressed a view that those in the top 1% of the global income distribution had benefited at the expense of the rest of society. For some this was relevant only as an explanation of the fall-out of the financial crisis, yet for many others it typified the way the economy had been transformed during the previous three decades. The Occupy movement highlighted the growth in economic inequality as one of the most distinctive elements of the neoliberal era. As a result, the topic became a subject of mainstream political debate – with few contesting the basic facts, merely their significance. It was such increased economic awareness that created the atmosphere in which Thomas Piketty's (2014) *Capital in the Twenty-first Century* could become such an unlikely bestseller – unlikely not simply because of its wink to Marx's *Capital* but also because it is far from an easy read, featuring an endless stream of data. Unlike Piketty and many of his followers, the Occupy movement never thought of the growth of inequality primarily as an issue for policymakers: it forcefully argued that policymaking itself has become skewed towards the interests of large corporations, and that, in the process, democracy has become hollowed out and unresponsive to the interests of ordinary people. This chapter takes up the issues of inequality, power and democracy and their relationship to neoliberalism.

Throughout this book we have argued that in order to gain a balanced perspective on the significance of neoliberalism, we need to both situate it as part of the long-term development of capitalism and appreciate the distinctive ways in which it has affected that development. We have been concerned to avoid viewing neoliberalism as a *sui generis* social formation – an approach characterized by the unfortunate view that the postwar era was a normative model of social and political justice. Yet we have also argued that neoliberalism presents a distinctive development in the history of capitalism and have sought to distinguish our account from the view that rejects the relevance of neoliberalism as a concept. This chapter argues that by increasing economic inequality, quarantining economic policy from democratic deliberation and magnifying the power of finance capital, neoliberalism leverages and amplifies some of capitalism's essential features, but does so in ways that are distinctive and set neoliberalism apart from previous forms of capitalist governance.

Power in capitalist society

As a prelude to our examination of the relationship between neoliberalism and inequality it is necessary to appreciate the specific way in which power operates in capitalist society more generally and how it generates economic inequality. The historical association between modern industrial capitalism and inequality is striking. If we draw on Angus Maddison's attempts to measure the development of GDP through history in different areas (Maddison Project 2013), we see that global inequality was very limited for a long time. Around 1500 – typically taken as the era when commercial dynamics began to push up against the institutions of feudalism – small differences among different regions start to appear. But only in the early nineteenth century, with the emergence of industrial capitalism, do we begin to see major differences arising, with Europe and North America becoming significantly wealthier than other areas. By the end of the century these differences have increased further, and they continued to do so during the twentieth century. Certainly such data are highly imprecise (after all, the concept of GDP is a modern invention), but they do establish beyond much reasonable doubt that the development of modern capitalism involved a significant increase in global inequality. Indeed, perhaps the most important factor the data leave out is the differences within countries, and bringing that factor in only reinforces the picture. Bourguignon and Morrison (2002: 727) point out that whereas the Gini-coefficient (which expresses the degree to which a given income distribution diverges from a situation of perfect equality – the higher the coefficient, the higher the number) for inequality between countries in 1820 was 0.16, the actual, global Gini-coefficient (which takes into account inequalities within countries) was far higher at 0.50. With the growth of industrial capitalism, the Gini-coefficient rose continuously for about a century, reaching 0.61 just before the First World War. Whereas in 1820 the poorest 40 per cent of the global population made 13.5 per cent of total world income, by 1910 that had gone down to 8.8 per cent. In the meantime, whereas in 1820 the world's richest 10 per cent had 42.8 per cent of the world's total income, by 1910 this had risen to 50.9 per cent (Bourguignon and Morrison 2002: 731, Table 1).

One of the most paradoxical aspects of capitalist life is the way in which equality and inequality intertwine: capitalism is characterized by a capacity for exploitation through incorporation, for oppression that works not through exclusion but precisely by integrating people into a framework of rights. Or, in the parlance of modern political theory, capital organizes 'exclusion through inclusion'. Of course that is not to deny that the institutional structures of capitalism may at times permit forms of oppression that are based on the flagrant violation of basic rights (such as slavery or racial discrimination), but in so far as capitalism is characterized by a distinctive dynamic of its own, this involves the organization of exploitation through a legal framework of private property. Capitalism has a distinctive way of promoting both political and legal forms of equality while at the same time driving the growth of distinctly economic forms of inequality. We can return here to Wood's (1995) description of capitalism in terms of the way it tends to institutionally differentiate political processes from economic ones. Under feudalism, power, distribution and class relations were directly political, more or less immediately backed up by force. The capitalist state, by contrast, is a constitutional state: it imposes limits on personal power and its arbitrary exercise. As a result, the economy, and social life more generally, acquire a certain autonomy from the state; people can enter into relationships and transactions of their own choosing as long as they respect formal principles of legal equality and private property. But the differentiation of the political and the economic under capitalism also means that power comes to operate in more indirect and structural ways. Power in capitalism reaches much further than in previous societies and tends to amplify inequalities in a way that no previous society did.

When it comes to the development of capitalism in European countries, above all England, the idea that formal equality goes hand in hand with substantive inequality received a very specific expression. This was how Marx thought about the significance of the transformation of feudal-agrarian forms of production into a system of industrial capitalism – that is, as a transformation of overtly political exploitation based on explicit status inequalities into a more pernicious form of inequality grounded in the formal exchange-based equality of the wage relationship. The growth of the capitalist market meant not just a liberation from dependence on feudal lords, but a separation from traditional forms of communal property that had provided access to non-market sources of subsistence (Wood 1995). Capitalists invested in new techniques that served to mechanize production processes and allowed for production on a mass scale. As work in factories increasingly took the place of agrarian and craft-based production, the result was the rise of massive industrial conglomerations. The sheer abundance of available labour put a downward pressure on wages, which industrialists were all too happy to exploit. During this time, inequalities within European countries began to grow dramatically (Engels 2009).

The notion of a shift from direct to more structural forms of power also gives us a conceptual handle on the dramatic growth in global inequality over the past two centuries. Until then, different regions largely developed by themselves, with whatever natural resources they had and the particular forms of social and political organization they had evolved. This certainly at times involved intense inequalities, but networks of power remained mostly local in character. The world as a whole was not systematically divided into rich and poor regions, or First vs. Third World, North vs. South, etc. Similarly, although imperialism existed well before the advent of industrial capitalism, the forms of imperialism that prevailed prior to that time did not have the same structural impact as they did later on (Wood 2005). As Stavrianos comments, 'precapitalist conquerors exploited their possessions simply and directly by plundering and by collecting tribute, chiefly in the form of foodstuffs. But this exploitation did not particularly affect the economic life and structure of the subject territories' (1981: 36). Capitalist forms of imperialism, by contrast, tend to effect a more basic shift in the social structure and operation of the colonized territory, inserting these regions into a global system on terms that serve to systematically increase inequalities (McNally 2006).

But at no point in the history of capitalism has this differentiation of politics from economics meant that the state became irrelevant. As Panitch and Gindin note, 'as capitalism developed states in fact became more involved in economic life than ever, especially in the establishment and administration of the juridical, regulatory and infrastructural framework in which private property, competition and contracts came to operate' (2012: 3). Yet the differentiation between the economic and political has an inevitable ideological dimension that diverts attention from the ways in which relations of power and authority become part of the structures that organize our everyday lives. Consequently, a logic of continuous state involvement operates alongside the image of a rigorous separation of public authority and the private sphere (Konings 2010). Nor, as we have argued, is this something that has escaped neoliberals, who have never been as fully captive to their formal ideological framework as critical theorists have at times liked to imagine. Often enough, neoliberal politicians and intellectuals are fully aware of the necessary role of the state in underpinning the market order – even if the political rhetoric on which they rely demonizes excessive state regulation of economic activity.

But the practical effects of this fiction of separation becomes apparent in the ways in which the capitalist economy has often been shielded from popular demands for democratic decision-making. Because of the differentiation between the political and economic spheres, democracy as it has developed under capitalism has been predominantly political, rather than economic, in nature. Thus, while democracy has grown alongside capitalism, it has always been limited in scope: it has remained a distinctively liberal, or formal, democracy, leaving decisions over production and investment in private hands and so leaving intact structural mechanisms for the production of inequality. One way of interpreting neoliberalism is as a reaction against the tendency of democratic pressures to transgress the limits imposed by liberal constitutionalism and as opposed to the demands by labour and social movements for the further extension of democratic principles into social and economic life.

As we argued in the introduction, neoliberalism is distinctive for its intuitive comfort with the dialectic of market freedom and market construction: it makes active use of the state even as its legitimacy remains bound up with an insistence on the separation of state and economy. In this way, it has been able to rekindle some of the more paradoxical characteristics of capitalism, renewing the dynamism of its distinctive mechanisms of inequality production. From the 1980s, transformations in the ways in which states regulated the economy, allied with the erosion of trade union power and the US-led imposition of structural adjustment programmes on the global South, combined to drive an enormous and lasting increase in economic inequality. Similarly, neoliberalism has effectively entailed a reassertion of imperialist relations, but with qualitatively new and distinct methods – primarily the process of structural adjustment and conditional lending as rolled out by the IMF and World Bank, both of which are dominated by the interests of the core capitalist states (Kiely 2007).

Inequality in historical perspective

The ways in which capitalism engenders inequality have never gone unchallenged. During the nineteenth century, with the rise of industrial capitalism, class conflict became ever more significant. As workers were concentrated in cities and working under the same roof, it became easier for them to organize, even though their efforts were met with tremendous political resistance from elites. We should bear in mind here that during this time political systems were far from democratic: the democratization of political structures (most prominently through universal [male] franchise) was itself one of the key objectives of the labour movement (Bendix 1977). An organized movement emerged towards the end of the nineteenth century: workers won the right to organize in unions and socialist parties were founded across Europe; and ultimately they won the right to vote. This expansion of citizenship rights meant that the liberal state was transformed into a liberal-democratic state. Workers used the franchise to push for things like a minimum wage, workplace regulations, unemployment insurance, etc., in effect demanding significant redistribution and pushing for the transformation of the liberal-democratic state into a social-democratic one (Sassoon 1996).

These demands for redistribution came at the same time as capitalist growth was slackening: the rate at which the economy was growing was slowing down, and it was becoming harder and harder to deny the working class a larger share of the economic surplus. These circumstances became a major factor in the acceleration of imperialist expansion: the late nineteenth century saw an extraordinary scramble for colonies, and areas that had hitherto been largely unaffected by the growth of capitalism now became more integrated into its dynamics (Hobsbawm 1989). This entailed a redistribution of global resources from Africa and Asia to Western Europe and a huge rise in global inequality. It also exacerbated inter-imperial rivalry, which has often been seen as one of the key factors behind geopolitical instability. That instability was given a boost by the onset of the Great Depression, to which Western countries responded by resorting to protectionism, cutting themselves off from Western markets and relying more and more on the exploitation of their colonial territories. The rise of nationalism prepared the ground for the rise of fascism and the collapse of Western liberalism (Kindleberger 1989).

The situation after the Second World War was significantly different from that after the First. Instead of another descent into chaos, what emerged was a global capitalist order characterized by a much greater capacity to distribute its benefits and integrate ordinary people into its dynamics. Consequently it enjoyed a much higher degree of legitimacy. This was the institutional context out of which the neoliberal policy revolution would eventually emerge, so it is important to understand its distinct dynamics and their relationship to inequality. The postwar hegemony of the US oversaw a reconstruction of imperialism. The way European countries had sought to reinforce colonial domination during the interwar period had provoked major resistance, resulting in national liberation struggles and decolonization movements. Many of these movements initially looked to the Soviet Union for ideological and material support, and the US (which did not itself have colonial possessions) was concerned to counter Soviet influence by drawing these movements into the capitalist hemisphere (Hobsbawm 1996). Aside from material and logistical assistance, a key ingredient in America's attempt to maintain influence in the decolonizing regions was the promise that if their revolutions were to take the capitalist rather than the communist route they could count on integration into the global capitalist order. Here we find the origins of the 'development project' (see McMichael 2012): the idea that capitalism could work to make prosperity available everywhere and that the goal for Southern countries was to reach a level of development comparable to that of the Western world.

During the 1950s and 1960s there was a great degree of optimism about the future of the developing world, premised upon the belief that the benefits of capitalism could be universalized (e.g., Rostow 1960). 'Dependency theorists' questioned such assumptions, arguing that the underdevelopment of the South needed to be seen as the flipside of the development of the North (Frank 1978; Cardoso and Faletto 1979). Their argument was that a structure of dependent development was in place that the expansion of capitalism would only reinforce. The effect of that expansion had been to lock the periphery into a structural dependency on the production of a few particular products, with little prospect for industrialization and the development of manufacturing industries. These theorists discerned a new kind of 'transnational' capitalism that reinforced the effects of this dependency and undermined the prospects of developing countries. Their argument was that developing countries may have freed themselves from colonialism *politically* but that *economically* they were becoming subject to a growing dependence.

In this context – at the point where political independence was secure but the effects of economic dependence were being increasingly felt – Southern countries began to push for what came to be known as a 'New International Economic Order' (Hudson 2005). Demands and objectives included more favourable terms of trade, the reduction of Western tariffs, and the stricter regulation of Western multinational corporations. Essentially what Southern countries demanded was more scope for autonomous development.

At the same time, in Western countries, optimism about the new alliance between capitalism and democracy was giving way to a growing discontent with the limitations of the welfare state and social democracy, which gave rise to industrial militancy and political radicalization (Panitch 1976; Crouch 1977). At a time when capitalism was entering a period of slowdown and growing international competition, working classes and popular movements began to make more radical demands. In the context of full employment and strong unions, demands for higher wage rises in particular posed a major threat to capital. All this meant renewed political tensions between labour and capital, the declining viability of the institutions of the social-democratic welfare state, and an erosion of the social compromise that had underpinned it.

The conflicts generated by such processes provided the context for the roll-out of neoliberalism. And yet, neoliberalism was not simply imposed 'from above'. Since the Second World War, the Western population had become much more deeply integrated into capitalism. We tend to think of the welfare state as providing the working classes with a degree of independence from the capitalist labour market, and although this is true in some respects, such overly nostalgic depictions of the postwar order nonetheless fail to recognize that, more fundamentally, the postwar compromise meant that the working class was participating in and legitimating the capitalist order. Their structural dependence on capitalist institutions had increased, and, to a certain extent at least, large sections of society had come to view capitalism's problems as their own problems, making them more receptive to policies that sought to restore the conditions of capitalist growth. This 'structural dependency' – a concept typically used in discussions of development but quite appropriate for describing the domestic dynamics in Northern countries during the 1970s – was what neoliberalism managed to leverage (Panitch and Gindin 2012; Konings 2011). Politicians like Thatcher and Reagan were able to break the political stalemate of the 1970s by convincing enough people that too many of the institutions of the postwar order (unions, the welfare state, and more general economic demands on government) were preventing the capitalist market from working properly. Essentially what elites managed to do in the 1970s and 1980s that they had not been able to do during the early twentieth century was reconstruct capitalist relations of exploitation and renew the vitality of capitalism without escalating political conflict.

This brings us back to a consideration of neoliberalism and democracy. Neoliberal intellectuals have always had an ambivalent relationship with democracy. As they are primarily concerned with economic logics, democracy is often viewed as a second-order priority, rather than an end in itself – indeed, the market freedom of private property is viewed as a precondition for any viable democracy. Central to the public choice strand of neoliberalism, for example, is a critique of democratic institutions as favouring the interests of politicians and bureaucrats, leading public choice theorists to emphasize the need to limit the policy autonomy of democratic governments. Such ambivalence was richly on display in the reactions of leading neoliberal intellectuals to the Pinochet dictatorship in Chile, which both Friedman and Hayek visited. While Friedman expressed reservations about the coercive nature of the Chilean regime, he was impressed with the direction of economic reform and met with Pinochet in 1975, subsequently advising the dictator, via correspondence, on economic policy. Hayek was more consistently supportive in his assessment, writing in a letter to the London *Times* that 'I have not been able to find a single person even in much maligned Chile who did not agree that personal freedom was much greater under Pinochet than it had been under Allende' (in Farrant and McPhail 2014: 332).

Some of its most prominent critics have tended to view this episode as revealing an essential truth about neoliberalism (e.g., Mirowski 2013). From such a perspective, neoliberalism is above all authoritarian, committed to bypassing and rolling back democratic institutions. In this book we have highlighted some of the ways in which neoliberal policies undermine or threaten democratic processes. For instance, we have identified several of the new mechanisms through which large corporations have come to make public policy, which has led Susan George (2015) to describe them as 'shadow sovereigns'. However, although neoliberalism was in large part a reaction against the radical democratic demands emanating from the social movements of the 1960s and 1970s, we should treat the idea that neoliberalism has essentially been about de-democratization with some caution, for several reasons. First, it is hard to deny that liberal democracy has flourished under neoliberalism: more governments are now formally democratic than at the beginning of the neoliberal era (Ayers and Saad-Filho 2015). Second, neoliberalism has never been simply predicated on depoliticization, in the sense of an absence of political protest or an active, willing endorsement of neoliberal ideology. One of its more paradoxical features is how it has often been able to capitalize on crises and the kind of political discontent they engender – even when neoliberal policies themselves are widely held responsible for the problems in the first place. This is its ability to 'fail forward' (Peck 2010: 6). Third, the focus on de-democratization can also lead to a somewhat nostalgic view of the postwar era as a golden age of democracy and social justice, turning a blind eye to some of the serious gender- and race-based oppressions that sustained that order. In the US case, for instance, the neoliberal agenda has never sought simply to reverse the gains of the Civil Rights movement but has rather re-founded racial oppression on new mechanisms (Wilson 1997; Kozol 2006). Often enough, the key strength of neoliberalism has been its ability to organize exclusion through inclusion – rolling back the substantive gains of democracy without eradicating formal democratic institutions. In this sense, neoliberalism entails leveraging some of capitalism's basic institutional features in new and historically specific ways.

Neoliberal inequality in the West

In previous chapters we have examined some of the key processes of neoliberal restructuring and their effects. We are now in a position to show the impact of neoliberalism on inequality and to underline its character as a system of power and control. Central to this process has been the role of finance, and the way this has interacted with trends in the 'real economy' (Bengtsson and Ryner 2015). As international competition intensified from the 1960s, US manufacturing, as we have seen, came under significant pressure, leading to a decline in its employment share. The dramatic increase in interest rates during the early 1980s that followed the Volcker shock lured large amounts of capital away from industrial investment and so gave additional impetus to the process of manufacturing decline. The same trend has been visible across the Western world.

The process of deindustrialization has been uneven and has affected different regions in different ways, depending on the specific character and configuration of the existing industry. A well-known example of dramatic and wholesale urban decline is Detroit, Michigan. Between the 1980s and 2015, US manufacturing shed 7 million jobs, which represented a contraction of 36.1 per cent (BIS 2016). During the heyday of Fordism, Detroit was known as the Motor City: a major centre of car production, much of the city's economic and social infrastructure was dependent on this industrial base. The decline of the American auto industry hit Detroit extremely hard: manufacturing employment was decimated, and the city's population is currently less than half what it once was. All this had a pronounced geographical and racial dimension, with unemployment and poverty concentrated at particularly high rates in neighbourhoods populated by African-Americans (Sugrue 2014).

This trend of deindustrialization, combined with the decline in trade union density and power, the growth of precarious work and wage stagnation, led to growing levels of inequality, as expressed in a steadily rising Gini index. Over the period 1979–2011, the income of the bottom 80 per cent of Americans grew by 16 per cent (adjusted for inflation) (CBO 2011: 18, figure 8). Over the same period, the US economy grew by 230 per cent (also adjusted for inflation) (Federal Reserve Bank of St. Louis 2017). As the OECD (2012) reports, the trend of a falling wage share in national income could be found in almost all of its member states. As discussed in Chapter 3, at the same time as the world of work was being restructured, states made significant cutbacks in existing arrangements for public income provision. As wages stagnated and public sources of income became harder to access, demand for credit grew dramatically. A growing share of this was in the form of 'non-revolving debt' such as credit card borrowing, which one can maintain by making regular payments on the interest while leaving the principal in place (Montgomerie 2009). Mortgage loans were often used by people to cash out some of the (often imagined) surplus value in their home. Whereas total US consumer debt in 1978 was $263 billion, by 1990 it had risen to $798 billion. It grew further to $1,539 billion in 2000 and to $3,330 billion in 2015

(Board of Governors of the Federal Reserve System 2017). Low-income Americans also became increasingly reliant on payday loans, which provide high-interest credit to those who are unable to make it through the month on what they take home in wages (Soederberg 2014). Although in principle such loans are meant to tide people over until payday, in practice they often quickly draw people into a series of rapidly growing loans, due to the accumulating interest. As McLean (2016) points out, by 2008 the US had more payday loan branches than McDonald's restaurants. Marston and Shevellar (2014) capture the increasing reliance on payday loans in terms of a 'shadow welfare state', to highlight the degree to which their growth has been driven by the need for non-wage sources of income that were once provided by public schemes. During the neoliberal era, debt has become a staple of life in many Western countries, above all in the US and the UK. It has been a key modality of the 'poverty industry' (Hatcher 2016): Wall Street's ability to make money off the growing precarity of 'Main Street'. The financial technique of securitization, examined in Chapter 2, was crucial here, as it allowed small, ordinary loans to be repackaged into assets that could be traded on financial markets.

Mainstream commentators have often seen the dramatic expansion of credit in terms of the democratization of finance (Shiller 2004). Although the analysis advanced here suggests that this is a highly one-sided and problematic perspective on the financialization process (see also Erturk et al. 2007), it is nonetheless important to appreciate what such interpretations tell us about the functions that the expansion of finance fulfils. To a significant extent, the social unrest of the 1960s and 1970s was driven by the struggles of minorities and oppressed groups to gain access to the benefits of welfare capitalism from which they had hitherto been excluded. Among the key demands of progressive reform movements during that era was that women and ethnic minorities should be able to access credit. One of the main reasons why it was so difficult for financial authorities to stem inflation by clamping down on financial innovation and credit creation was that restrictions on the latter very quickly translated into a decreased availability of credit at a time when its expansion was crucial to social and political stability. The Volcker shock altered some of the key parameters here, allowing financial expansion to proceed without causing consumer price inflation. Neoliberal policies have in fact made credit far more widely available than ever before, but far from this being an egalitarian development, it has had all the characteristics of a paradoxical process of exclusion through inclusion. The intertwining of credit and poverty has often trapped people in cycles of growing debt. Oxfam speaks of a 'finance curse': while often welcome as a source of employment and profits, a large financial sector tends to correlate with high levels of inequality and poverty (Oxfam 2016: 25).

It is important to appreciate that economic inequality has major consequences in areas of human life that we do not normally think of as economic. Increases in unemployment as a result of economic crises lead to higher rates of chronic illness and mortality, higher rates of mental health problems in affected families (including the children), and the increased use of addictive stimulants like alcohol and tobacco (Bambra et al. 2016: 165). Cuts in public services in times of fiscal austerity tend to hit the poorest sections of the populations hardest, exacerbating existing disparities in healthcare and outcomes (Bambra et al. 2016: 169). Similarly, neoliberal restructuring has had a profound impact on educational opportunities and achievements. This is perhaps most obvious in the escalating cost of tertiary tuition across much of the Western world (especially in the US), which means that access to educational opportunities is increasingly tied to parental income and wealth. But there is a more subtle process at work here as well: from the start, children from families in higher socioeconomic brackets tend to perform better in school systems that have been reorganized along neoliberal lines, such as through the introduction of continuous testing and standardized curricula, and this then feeds into wider disparities later on. The way in which neoliberal policies have affected the role of education in contemporary society means that it functions less and less as a vehicle of equal opportunity and more and more as a means of transmitting inequalities across generations (Kozol 2012). In a way that is oddly feudal, the educational opportunities afforded by one's parents' socioeconomic status are the very means by which one secures one's own ability to stay in that bracket.

Neoliberalism, inequality and the developing world

If the changing relationship between industry and finance was central to the construction of a new, inegalitarian regime in Western countries, this was no less the case for the global situation. We have already seen the degree to which the changing relations between the North and the South were shaped by the debt crisis and the way this was compounded by the shift in American financial policy with the Volcker shock. To get a better sense of the magnitude of that shift, it is useful to look at some numbers. Whereas in 1970 Mexico's debt was $2.2 billion, by 1982 it had risen to $50.4 billion (Bulow and Rogoff 1990: 41, Table 3). Latin America's total debt grew from $15.9 billion in the 1970s to $334.9 billion by 1988 – a twenty-fold increase in less than two decades. Africa's total debt, meanwhile, increased from $5.4 billion in 1970 to $112.4 billion in 1988 (Bradshaw and Huang 1991: 322, Table 1). As we have seen, these extraordinarily rapid increases in indebtedness provided the IMF and World Bank with a great deal of leverage, which they exploited to impose neoliberal restructuring programmes (Peet 2003). The official rationale for structural adjustment was to put in place institutions that would ensure the efficient operation of market principles and so allow countries to generate economic growth, earn foreign exchange, and work their way out of debt. But for all the claims to neutrality, in practice these interventions served to adjust the production structures of developing countries in ways that meant a return to historical patterns of specialization, with a heavy emphasis on exports of primary goods, raw materials and agrarian products. When all was said and done, that was simply the quickest way to earn the foreign exchange that would permit debt repayment. In this way, following a logic that had been correctly discerned by dependency theorists, Southern countries were cut off from opportunities for independent economic development and forced to return to colonial patterns of economic specialization.

At the same time, the austerity programmes imposed by the IMF and the World Bank not only entailed a direct reduction of public services, but also had a depressing effect on domestic demand, which put further pressure on domestic industries. The result was not simply a further turn towards exports, but also the creation of a massive supply of cheap labour that could be exploited by Western multinational corporations now that restrictions on foreign direct investment had mostly been lifted. As noted in Chapter 4, since the 1970s flows of foreign direct investment have increased exponentially. Moreover, in the new context in which independent economic development seemed out of reach, actively working to attract foreign capital by offering favourable investment conditions became a key objective of many Southern countries. The degree to which this has in practice come down to offering favourable conditions for the exploitation of the domestic labour force has been evident in the creation of so-called 'special economic zones', where Western corporations can operate exempt from many of the legal and regulatory obligations that would normally apply. Many Southern countries thus transformed themselves into labour-intensive, low-cost and low-wage producers for industrialized countries.

These developments have done much to drive the growth of global inequality since the late 1970s. If it is too crude to summarize the relationship between neoliberalism and global restructuring by saying that finance capital held a gun to the head of the developing world while industrial capital went in and emptied the safe, this nonetheless captures something of the efficiency with which the international financial institutions have leveraged the debt crisis to effect an extraordinary redistribution of resources from the South to the North. During the 1980s, per capita GDP in sub-Saharan Africa decreased by an annual rate of 0.96 per cent, and per capita GDP in Central and South America contracted at an annual rate of 0.77 per cent. During the same decade, per capita GDP in industrial economies grew at an annual rate of 2.16 per cent (Berry and Serieux 2006: 6). Whereas the growth of global inequality had flattened off somewhat during the postwar period, it now increased again. As Milanović (2009: 18, Table 3) reports, the global Gini index increased from 0.64 in 1960 to 0.66 in 1980 and increased further to 0.71 in 2002.

The damage wrought upon developing countries during the 1980s did not of course go unnoticed. The turn of the century saw a gradual transition from the identifiably neoliberal 'Washington Consensus' approach to a different model of development that was formulated during the 1990s and subsequently articulated in terms of the Millennium Development Goals. One of the characteristics of this new development framework is the importance it places not simply on attracting foreign capital but on possibilities for tapping into new sources of domestic entrepreneurialism. Microfinance is a good example here: it aims to make small loans available to poor people who would be unlikely to have sought or received a loan from a bank or who might not even have considered their skills to be a form of human capital that could be valorized. But microfinance has had difficulty living up to its promises. Roy traces its fairly rapid transformation from a philanthropic orientation into a business like many others, driven more by the profit objectives of Western lenders than the development needs of the global South. Indeed, she refers to microfinance as 'poverty capital': capital that seeks to make poverty profitable and 'to capture a key frontier: the poorest financial consumers or the "last billion"' (Roy 2010: 30). The practical workings of microfinance are thus situated between 'the financialization of development and the democratization of capital' (Roy 2010: 31). In many ways the Millennium Development framework put a much friendlier face on what nevertheless remained policies of neoliberal development (Soederberg 2005).

Another rather deceptive cause for optimism has been the argument, advanced by authors such as Milanović over the last decade or so, that the growth of global inequality has slowed down or even been reversed, due above all to the rapid growth of an economic 'middle class' in China and India. This has given rise to high hopes for what the ongoing development of these countries will mean for the reduction of global inequality in the future. As an op-ed headline in the *Washington Post* put it, 'Stop obsessing about inequality. It's actually decreasing around the world' (Tupy 2015). But even though China has made significant strides in reducing rural poverty, inequality has actually increased within the country as it has shifted from a predominantly agrarian peasant communist economy into a more neoliberal capitalist one in which millions of people have become newly dependent on waged work. In 2016, the *Financial Times*, not normally a publication easily alarmed by issues of inequality, reported on the extreme levels of income inequality in China, levels that are surpassed only by South Africa and Brazil (Wildau and Mitchell 2016).

The return of inequality into Western political discourse

Certainly one would be hard-pressed to view recent economic developments as evidence *against* the idea that capitalism is characterized by a structural tendency to generate inequality. Indeed, recent years have seen a growing awareness of the return of severe inequality and poverty in the West itself. The most well-known exponent of such concerns is Thomas Piketty, whose *Capital in the Twenty-first Century* (2014) documents at great length the increase in economic inequality over the past decades in Western countries. Although the theoretical merits of Piketty's work are hotly debated, there is one aspect in which his conceptual emphasis seems particularly appropriate, namely in his attention to the growing importance of wealth. Economists are used to making a distinction between inequality of income (flow) and inequality of assets (stock). So far in this chapter we haven't focused on this distinction because it stands to reason that ongoing inequalities in income will, if sustained year after year, have a cumulative effect that will generate asset inequalities. And since assets generate income, it also is hardly surprising that a certain self-reinforcing logic is at work here (i.e. the wealthy have more ways to maintain their wealth than the poor have ways to build it up). But in neoliberalism the distinction between income and assets has become more important: a key source of inequality in recent decades has been speculative capital gains, i.e. the appreciation of asset values.

To see how this works we should go back for a moment to the discussion of financialization. We tend to take it for granted that the commitment of central banks to targeting inflation naturally goes hand in hand with dynamic and expansionary financial markets. But of course this alliance is far from self-evident. During the 1970s financial policy-makers viewed the creation of credit through securitization techniques as being responsible for higher levels of inflation. Although inflation came down following the Volcker shock, it didn't do so as a result of curtailing financial innovation or dynamism. It involved a broader series of moves that isolated the consumer price index from the effects of financial market activity. The relentless inflation targeting of modern central banks is based on a distinction between assets and consumer items that is not politically neutral in terms of its distributional effects. This is most obvious with respect to house prices. From the perspective of many families, houses are an essential cost-of-living item, but they are not included (at least not fully) in the basket of goods in terms of which inflation is measured. For instance, a 2 per cent wage increase is likely to imply a lower standard of living if one lives in an area where house prices are going up at a rate of, say, 7 per cent a year – a figure that is hardly uncommon in many of the world's major cities. The only way to get out of this situation is to get into the market in order to benefit from the capital gains – but of course that requires a down-payment, and the downward pressure on wages prevents many from saving enough each month to raise the necessary funds. Increasingly, then, the possibility of getting on the 'property ladder' requires that one have assets to start out with, typically an inheritance (Cooper 2017). As Piketty points out, the neoliberal era has seen a pronounced return of the tendency for wealth to be transmitted across generations.

The dynamics of asset prices have thus been a major driver of inequality. Indicative of this is the dramatic increase in the number of billionaires: whereas globally in 1987 there were a total of 140 billionaires, by 2014 this had increased to a total of 1,645 (Di Muzio 2015: 502). With the benefit of hindsight, it is beginning to seem as if the relatively egalitarian societies constructed in Western countries during the first three decades after the Second World War were in key respects exceptional – the outcome not of capitalist development itself, but of the intense struggles it had triggered and of the need to meet popular demands in order to maintain legitimacy and forestall revolution. The widespread discussion that Piketty's findings have provoked speaks to a growing anxiety among Western elites about the issue of inequality and the emerging awareness that it is not purely an economic phenomenon, but has profound social, political and even psychological impacts. There is a renewed appreciation for the 'spirit level' (Wilkinson and Pickett 2011), and we are now regularly treated to claims that inequality is bad for society 'as a whole'. Even as faithful a supporter of all things capitalist as the consulting firm McKinsey recently issued a report highlighting the dangers of growing inequality. It worries that

> flat or falling incomes for the majority of the population could reduce demand growth and increase the need for social spending. Social consequences are also possible; in our survey, nearly a third of those who felt they were not advancing thought that their children and the next generation would also advance more slowly in the future, and they expressed negative opinions about trade and immigration. (McKinsey Global Institute 2016: viii)

Assessments such as these are concerned about the growth of poverty and inequality for rather instrumental reasons – that is, it is not seen as a problem in itself, but only when it begins to threaten the social institutions that produce it – and it is therefore not all that surprising that they have failed to have a significant impact on the political agenda. But it is far from clear that the willingness of elites to pay lip-service to the problem will be sufficient to prevent social contradictions from translating into more serious political challenges.

6
Crisis and Resilience

When Syriza, a coalition of left-wing parties, won the Greek parliamentary elections in January 2015 and formed a government, it carried with it the hopes of many that its anti-austerity platform would mark the beginning of the roll-back of neoliberalism within the European Union. The Greek government had been caught up in the sovereign-debt crisis precipitated by the financial contagion that spread through the global economy after the crash of 2007–8. Since 2010, Greece had been subject to successive 'bailouts', or 'economic adjustment programmes', negotiated with the EU and IMF. The packages extended credit to Greece to pay the large financial institutions who were its main creditors, while requiring the government to implement a radical austerity agenda, including privatization as well as cuts to social services, government spending and a range of social protections. Yet, the Greek economy continued to spiral downwards as aggregate demand tanked on the back of the austerity programme, with unemployment climbing to over 25 per cent, while the cost of government borrowing sky-rocketed.

Syriza's victory in the 2015 elections came on the back of its explicitly anti-neoliberal platform in which it promised to tear up the austerity agreements. After the leaders of Germany and France, the European Central Bank and the IMF refused to write off Greek debt and consider alternatives to austerity, the Syriza government called a referendum on the matter in

July 2015, in which 61 per cent of Greek voters registered their opposition to the austerity package. When the EU, ECB and IMF still refused Greece's request, the Greek Prime Minister eventually accepted a revised austerity package, causing a split within Syriza. What loomed as an existential crisis for neoliberalism was transformed into its rebirth. That one of the most identifiably anti-neoliberal governments the world has witnessed would U-turn on its professed commitments, even when backed by a popular mandate, points to the resilience of neoliberalism. It prompts consideration of whether the current crisis heralds its demise or its reinvention, an issue which will be taken up in this chapter.

Neoliberalism has never lacked critics who have pointed to its tendency to generate crises and instability. It is important to appreciate why this argument features so prominently in the critique of neoliberalism. After all, we might well say that even if neoliberalism was a perfectly stable system, there would be enough left to be concerned about, notably its tendency to generate inequality, hardship and social dislocation. Indeed, much of this book, even as it has been concerned to avoid a rush to judgement, has been critical along such lines, and it has investigated the morally questionable and undemocratic sources of the growth of neoliberal policy models and the often extreme inequalities they have generated. But social scientists are understandably concerned to ground their critiques in criteria that are not simply reflective of a subjective value-judgement. Of course, one reason that neoliberalism creates instability no doubt has to do with the fact that it generates social and political dynamics that people find objectionable and therefore resist, so that the descriptive and the normative dimensions should never be fully separated. But critique, many appropriately feel, should nonetheless not *merely* reflect personal moral indignation.

As we have pointed out earlier, dynamics of crisis and instability seem to be most pronounced in financial life, which is why the critique of finance has always occupied such an important place in thinking about neoliberalism: it is here that it seems to fully manifest its objective impossibility as a totalizing logic and its lack of coherence as a basis for the organization of human society. But of course volatility is certainly not confined to the world of high finance. This is due in part to the ways in which the logic of finance has penetrated into everyday life – and it is worth noting here that theoretical work on the role of derivatives, initiated about a decade ago by authors such as LiPuma and Lee (2004) and Bryan and Rafferty (2006), has been taken up by scholars in cultural studies and security studies to illuminate the 'derivative' logic of different political, cultural and even artistic dimensions of neoliberal life and the ways in which it has infused them with new elements of volatility (see, e.g., the contributions to Lee and Martin 2016). But it is also because many crises are simply lived in ways that are not nearly as spectacular as full-scale financial meltdowns yet are no less injurious or incapacitating in their consequences. In such situations, to talk of a crisis means simply that existing ways of doing things have become unsustainable in a way that is impossible to ignore. Things simply cannot go on the way they have, and something has to give – change must occur, whether by design or default.

And yet, despite the undeniable tendency of neoliberalism to generate crises, it is still very much with us. Critics of neoliberalism have excelled at announcing or predicting its demise. But, notwithstanding the wish to find an objective ground for critique, it has remained rather unclear exactly what foundation or limit it is that neoliberalism violates or transgresses in a way that is not sustainable, in an onto-logically objective way. Indeed, this problem has been such a constant in the intellectual engagement with neoliberal-ism that we need to consider whether its ability to survive events that would appear to provide unambiguous grounds for declaring its demise is in fact a constitutive aspect of its modus operandi.

Neoliberal resilience after the crisis

Neoliberalism's capacity to survive events that would seem to demonstrate its essential incoherence has never been more obvious than in the aftermath of the global financial crisis. The crisis itself originated in a rather unexpected corner of the financial system. For years, it was primarily the spectacular dynamics of high finance that drew attention: the financial crises of the preceding decade had prominently involved currency speculation and stock market meltdowns, and during the first year of the twenty-first century it was above all the exploits of hedge funds and private equity funds that attracted concern and commentary. Scholars had certainly become interested in questions of securitization and the rapid growth of mortgage and credit card debt, but – notwithstanding the fact that many claimed to have 'predicted' the crisis – few commentators anticipated that the inability of a relatively small number of American homeowners to keep up with their mortgage payments could throw a major wrench into the wheels of global finance.

The crisis was immediately greeted as a major political game-changer. Some analyses were relatively cautious and simply pointed to the open-ended nature of the future. Others were far more optimistic and saw not only the end of neoliberalism but a welcome return to the days of the Keynesian welfare state and public regulation. Emboldened by the recent election of Barack Obama, Paul Krugman, in the introduction to the second edition of his book *The Conscience of a Liberal*, declared that 'The new New Deal starts now' (2009: xix). Krugman was hardly alone in making such predictions. In the political economy literature, anticipations of a return to a more civilized form of capitalism have become closely associated with a particular interpretation of the work of Polanyi, which sees history as moving in cycles of market disembedding and re-embedding. In this logic, markets tend to autonomize themselves from society, and the destructive consequences of this process trigger a response from society that seeks to re-embed financial forces in regulatory frameworks and social norms. The financial crisis was thus seen as a political turning point (Gills 2008; Wade 2008).

But as we have argued in this book, the idea that neoliberalism follows a logic of 'market disembedding' sets too much store by its ideological formulations and the way these are beholden to the notion of the 'free market'. Put differently, such approaches tend to view neoliberalism as simply a form of 'market fundamentalism' (Block and Somers 2014) and fail to fully appreciate its novelty – the way the practical rationality of its political project is shaped by the dialectic of market freedom and market construction. In so far as the Polanyian conceptual schema of disembedding and embeddedness has a certain purchase, it should be thought of in terms of that dialectical logic rather than as a cyclical theory of history. Neoliberalism was itself always embedded (Cahill 2014), and it is precisely such institutional embeddedness that has made the neoliberal order more durable than a pure market dystopia would be.

Expectations of a return to a more Keynesian policy consensus were initially buoyed when leading capitalist states effectively nationalized failing financial institutions – something almost unimaginable just a few years earlier – and announced wide-ranging fiscal stimulus packages. But the hopes for a renewal of the commitment to public protection were soon disappointed. In the US, the Obama administration managed to pass the American Recovery and Reinvestment Act and the Dodd-Frank Wall Street Reform and Consumer Protection Act, but already by that time concerns were widespread that it did relatively little to constrain Wall Street, not enough to help Main Street, and for all intents and purposes served to normalize the regime of too-big-to-fail expectations. Hopes for progressive legislation took a further hit when the Democrats lost the 2010 midterm elections, which emboldened Republicans to sabotage any Democratic attempts to rein in the financial sector. The Consumer Financial Protection Bureau, for instance, has had to fight for its life practically from the moment it was conceived, and has remained fairly powerless. But these developments not only dashed the hopes for a Polanyian countermovement, they amounted to a positive restoration of neoliberal policies that was particularly evident in the precipitous rise of austerity discourses, which targeted public debt as a major source of disorder and represented the antithesis of a Keynesian emphasis on the need for deficit spending amid a recession. What many predicted would be a post-neoliberal era has ended up looking and feeling very much like neoliberalism reloaded.

Nevertheless, there are certainly signs of the waning ability of neoliberalism to secure the conditions for economic growth, business profits and, in turn, political legitimacy. Warnings are being raised about the prospect of 'persistent stagnation' for the global economy, which has been torpid since 2009.

With the spectre of deflation looming, neither fiscal austerity nor accommodative monetary policy have been capable of reviving economic growth. It is in this context that key supranational institutions at the heart of the neoliberal project have themselves begun to question the wisdom of neoliberal policy. A recent report in the IMF's *Finance and Development* magazine, 'Neoliberalism: Oversold?', argued that the headline neoliberal policies of capital account liberalization and fiscal austerity had increased inequality which in turn depressed economic growth (Ostry, Loungani and Furceri 2016). And yet, neoliberal policies persist. Over the past few years, many scholars have grappled with the question of why neoliberalism failed to die, and how it is we are stuck with a system that generates so many undesirable consequences, a system that appeared to enjoy so little legitimacy only a few years ago. What then is the source of neoliberalism's resilience? The answers to this question that have gained the most traction centre on the role of the corporate and financial elites who have the most to gain from the continuation of neoliberal policies. In such interpretations, elites have been able to foil moves for reform through their iron-fisted hold on the institutions, norms and discourses of policymaking – through 'regulatory' or even 'cognitive capture' (Baker 2010; McCarty 2013).

But such explanations, popular as they are, are problematic. Of course, the role of elites has no doubt been an important factor in preventing popular grievances from translating into politically effective messages, as well as preventing any change at the level of institutional politics that did occur from translating into a durable change of policy. How true this was could be seen in the US, where even commonsensical proposals met with enormous resistance right from the start. The proposal for a law regulating proprietary trading (essentially it would have imposed some restrictions on banks' ability to mix up their own money with that of their clients, not unlike the New Deal's Glass-Steagall separation of commercial and investment banking), which was proposed by Paul Volcker, the man who had played such a crucial role in the neoliberalization of finance yet had come to feel that things may have got out of hand, was quickly painted as the idea of an inexpert crank and never stood a real chance. A version of it did get passed, but was so watered-down and riddled with exemptions that in practice it has imposed few constraints on the banks. A reading of Sheila Bair's (2013) account of her years at the Federal Deposit Insurance Corporation bears this point out quite concretely: her willingness to take on entrenched interests was actively fought by other often more powerful regulatory actors such as Treasury Secretary Tim Geithner, who, in their wish to promote stability and get the system back on track, were generally hostile to any initiatives that might challenge the ability of key financial actors to resume operations.

Yet it is not clear that the theory of 'regulatory capture' can stand on its own as an explanation for the failure of neoliberalism to expire. The power of elites is itself a function of the continued viability of neoliberal institutions and discourses, so to say that it was simply their power that prevented the demise of neoliberalism runs the risk of being somewhat tautological or uninformative. It does not account for the structural conditions that have allowed neoliberalism to escape what seemed an inevitable fate. The question that needs answering is precisely how elites could continue to access such tremendous material, institutional, symbolic and other resources even in a context where discontent with key neoliberal institutions was at an all-time high and the political air was thick with contempt for and distrust of bankers (cf. Kiersey 2011: 25).

It is worth noting here that regulatory capture is a distinctly neoliberal theory, first proposed by George Stigler (1971), a founding member of the Mont Pelerin Society. The theory imagines the market as providing its own, self-sufficient regulatory device and views politics and policy as undesirable intrusions and impositions that inevitably invite tendencies to rent-seeking (that is, attempts to curtail competition and use public resources for private interests). It understands undesirable outcomes not as organically rooted in economic and political structures, but as resulting from the corruption of an ideal state of affairs. In this way, it imagines a form of public policy that is neutral, and assesses actually existing policies against that image. Present-day critics of neoliberalism are of course motivated by a very different conception of the relationship between politics and markets, but what they have imported along with the theory of regulatory capture is the assumption of the principal neutrality of public policy. Many tend to assess post-crisis events against a normative image of the role of policy and then conceptualize actual events as a corruption or undesirable deviation from that image. In this way, their explanations have had a strongly negative flavour: they are more concerned to explain why something that should have happened (a turn away from neoliberalism) failed to happen than they are to explain what has actually happened. The upshot of this is that the problem of the persistence of neoliberalism comes to appear as a discrete policy problem traceable to specific interests or the influence of specific ideas, a problem that thus allows for correspondingly discrete solutions. What then disappears from view, as we have noted elsewhere in this book, are the structural dynamics of capitalism and the deeply embedded nature of neoliberalism.

Neoliberal reason and resilience

It is worth considering the concept of resilience a little further. So far we have used the concept in a somewhat imprecise sense, equating it generally with survival or continued existence. But the idea of resilience is often used to refer to something distinctive that is not captured by such phrases; namely, the ability to bounce back from failure, the ability not simply to ward off external challenges but to engage with and adapt to them. In other words, it refers to a dynamic quite different from that captured in the traditional, rather static, conceptions of order, stability and security. Notions of resilience are premised on the awareness that the idea of a riskless existence is a fantasy, and that the maintenance of human and social life principally involves not stasis but continuous adaptation to changing circumstances. In other words, the idea of resilience relates to the creation of order not by overriding risk or keeping it at bay, but by directly engaging with contingency and volatility.

This way of thinking is alien to neoclassical economics, which relies on a static notion of order. We should therefore bear in mind the point made in earlier chapters, that neo-liberalism goes well beyond neoclassical notions of equilibrium and mechanical notions of how markets operate. This is particularly evident in the Austrian strain of neoliberal theory, which stressed the role of markets as mechanisms for adjustment that allow for processes of endogenous self-organization and the evolutionary emergence of institutions that could never have been designed by a central authority. Already in the socialist calculation debate, Hayek readily acknowledged that if neoclassical economics offered an accurate representation of economic life – that is, if economic action was rational and operated under conditions of perfect information – then a centrally planned economy would have been perfectly possible. The reason that socialism was an inherently flawed project, however, was the fact that positivist assumptions about information and knowledge were deeply problematic. Human minds are not capable of attaining the kind of totalizing view that would permit perfect knowledge of the world, and uncertainty is therefore the necessary condition of economic action. In other words, risk and contingency are ineradicable. Failure to appreciate this, Hayek and his fellow Austrian economists argued, was at the root of the totalitarian fantasies that socialism had in common with fascism. Hayek (1988) would later frame this more philosophically in terms of the 'fatal conceit' of reason, which consisted in its inability to be cognizant of and observe its own limitations.

This meant that Hayek had a particular relationship to the classic liberal tradition that is reflective of the distinctiveness of neoliberalism. Although mainstream economic thought takes the classic economic liberalism of Adam Smith as its key point of reference, this amounts to little more than an article of faith: the whole point of its positivist and empiricist methodological orientation is to rule out the possibility of an 'invisible hand'. But Hayek's emphasis on the limits of human reason found its complement in an appreciation of the role of self-organizing mechanisms in human life, ways of ordering that are not rationally designed by any particular mind but that emerge as the unintended effects of the interaction of millions of individual plans. To locate the sources of capitalist order at that level of human interaction means that they cannot be reduced to purely rational evaluations. We might understand Hayek's perspective on economic order as a more secularized version of Smith's notion of the invisible hand: although Hayek was deeply indebted to that idea, he nonetheless felt that Smith's conception had remained 'metaphorical and incomplete' (1988: 148). The metaphor of the invisible hand reflected an important intuition of the principle of spontaneous ordering, but to Hayek's mind it still smacked too much of a belief in divine trickery. Hayek categorically denies the possibility of outside intervention or steering and views the emergence of economic order as driven by nothing but trial and error, uncertainty and discovery.

Whereas Smith advanced his famous metaphor in order to address the question of how order might still be possible in a secularizing world that can no longer see itself as governed by a divine mind, Hayek proposed his understanding of spontaneous self-organization not to address a concern about the limitations of secular reason but precisely in response to its 'conceit'; namely, the faith in rationalist constructivism that he saw as the defining characteristic of twentieth-century socialism and progressivism. His claim was not just that acting amid uncertainty was acceptable but that it was necessary, that there is no source of order other than in the active engagement with risk. This meant that Hayek's understanding of economic ordering as an unintended process shows striking resemblances with notions of self-organization and resilience in contemporary systems theory, cybernetics and brain science (Walker and Cooper 2011). Even if ordering is beyond rational and intentional human control, human actions are always already shaping this process, creating something that they were incapable of comprehending in real-time. Hayek's project is thus constructivist, committed to the idea that it can and must provoke the change that it wants to see in the world (Mirowski 2013).

Without wishing to imply a causal relationship between the two, this is in fact a fairly good description of the event that this book has emphasized as one of the key moments in the making of neoliberalism – the Volcker shock. Volcker himself did not set much store by the theoretical claims of monetarism as these had been expounded by Milton Friedman. That is, he did not share Friedman's conviction that money could be neatly defined and measured or that its quantity could be fixed in a straightforward way by central banks. But he felt that the growing influence of monetarist ideas – including in Congress – created a particular opportunity for administering the kind of shock therapy that he considered necessary to defeat the inflationary momentum that was sustained by the logic of expectations (i.e., the anticipation of inflation led unions to demand compensatory wage rises that were themselves inflationary). In other words, Volcker's move was a provocation, undertaken without a clear view of its likely consequences; it was speculative, driven by the hope that it would set in motion wider adjustments. He would not be disappointed: the turn to monetarism changed some of the key parameters of the US political economy. It is worth recalling here that Reagan himself was initially displeased with Volcker's policies and perceived them as obstacles to his political agenda. As Silber (2012) argues, Volcker's policies were critical in pushing Reagan to adopt the policies that we have since come to think of as 'Reaganism'.

As we have seen earlier, the turn to monetarism was a defining moment in the making of neoliberalism not because it brought the world in line with the image of a static equilibrium or a narrow interpretation of the efficient markets hypothesis. The Volcker shock did not conquer inflation by suppressing speculation or constraining the creation of money and credit. Indeed, it gave a dramatic boost to such processes. Financial innovation accelerated and expanded, producing inflationary pressures that were if anything stronger than during the 1970s. But these forces operated in a significantly altered institutional environment where such pressures primarily fed the inflation of asset prices and had become consistent with a non-inflationary environment for consumer goods (Konings 2011).

We can look at this as a process of financialization, but, as discussed earlier, we should be careful not to view it simply as a dysfunctional expansion of unproductive capital at the expense of real production. We should not be too quick to dismiss the possibility that financialization was more than a patch to cover up the underlying contradictions of capital. Rather, financialization has been characterized by its own distinctive dynamics and has allowed the logic of capital to penetrate more deeply into the fabric of human life and to uncover new sources of value. At work here is what we have earlier referred to, following Leyshon and Thrift (2007), as 'the capitalization of almost everything', that is, the possibility of constituting an ever expanding range of human capacities as financial assets that promise to deliver a stream of payments. These considerations should serve to caution against the widespread tendency to view the expansion of finance through neoliberalism as inherently unproductive: the growth of financial capital has been accompanied by the expansion of capacities for its valorization. As ever greater arenas of social life become subject to the logic of financial calculation this dynamic certainly has destructive tendencies. Yet it is precisely this ability to render social processes calculable that creates new avenues for profitable returns and from which the resilience of the financial dimension of neoliberalism stems.

The paradoxical politics of neoliberalism

However, resilience should not be considered exclusively from an economic point of view. From a more political perspective, it has to do primarily with the ability of neoliberal policy regimes and discourses to survive or even thrive on events that would seem to have done irreparable damage to their legitimacy. For critics like Mirowski, this speaks to neoliberalism's 'exceptional' nature: its survival being grounded in the possibility of suspending the rules and norms of liberal democracy at times of crisis. This has led critics to assume that the survival of neoliberalism is bound up with the possibility of heavy-handed state interventions at moments of full-blown crisis. On that reading, the neoliberal advocacy of the market is little more than a cynical subterfuge to legitimate the deployment of state power in the interests of corporate and financial elites. That is not always a bad depiction, and there are certainly times when neoliberalism primarily seems to be about the naked exercise of power in the interests of the few (here it is not just the alliance with military power evident in the Chile coup that comes to mind, but also the shock therapy that was key to the transition to neoliberalism in Eastern Europe, and we might even see the no-questions-asked bailouts during the financial crisis through a similar lens). But we have also seen that as a general depiction of neoliberalism such emphasis on its authoritarian, undemocratic aspects is misleading or at least insufficiently capacious, certainly when it comes to the need to make sense of its unexpected resilience in recent years in Europe and North America, where formal or liberal democracy has hardly been side-lined.

Neoliberalism may have had a deleterious effect on democracy in its substantive sense (Brown 2015), but we should be careful to distinguish this from older claims about the colonization of the political by the economic (Habermas 1975; Offe 1984). If neoliberalism has hollowed out democratic institutions in important ways, it is not clear that it has crowded out politics and political contestation in any meaningful sense. Indeed, one of the most notable developments since the financial crisis has been the growth of popular movements outside the framework of liberal democracy. And if we should certainly pay attention to the ways in which they have challenged neoliberalism, it is equally important to understand how popular politics have often been implicated in its maintenance. That is, rather than simply rejecting neoliberalism as an undemocratic project, we should be attuned to the way in which it has been capable of producing its own sources of legitimacy, and the ways in which the idea of 'getting the state out of the market' still has a pronounced popular appeal that confers on the neoliberal project a definite ideological strength.

Developments since the financial crisis have been highly paradoxical (Judis 2016). The popular resistance and instability triggered by the crisis was at a scale unseen during the previous decades. The Occupy Wall Street movement started in New York but soon spread to other cities in the US and elsewhere. The preceding years had seen a proliferation of the effects of the crisis, which included a drop in house prices (so that many people now owed more on their homes than they were worth), higher levels of unemployment, and the decimation of people's retirement savings. The growing economic precarity among ordinary Americans did not seem to be matched by similar levels of misfortune in the world of high finance: even as no relief was in sight for the US economy as a whole, bonuses in the financial sector were once again on the increase. Particularly glaring was the discrepancy between the government's willingness to guarantee the value of the financial securities that were backed by mortgages and its reluctance to put substantial resources behind helping out homeowners who had seen the value of their properties plummet.

But Occupy Wall Street was by no means the only response to the instability set in motion by the crisis. A very different response came from another popular movement – the Tea Party, which was a driving force behind the radicalization of the Republican Party that did so much to derail Obama's plans for reform. When the Obama administration announced the creation of a programme to help homeowners faced with the threat of foreclosure, it drew the ire of CNBC reporter Rick Santelli, who on air expressed outrage that the administration was 'rewarding bad behavior' and using public funds for yet more bailouts. With reference to colonial Americans' resistance to the punitive taxes levied by the British state, Santelli urged the nation's true 'capitalists' to start a 'tea party' to protest this assault on freedom (quoted in Skocpol and Williamson 2012: 7). This call for a new Tea Party quickly proved to have huge resonance: it appealed to many who had first been disappointed with the Bush administration's decision to bail out Wall Street and then appalled by the election of a Democratic President who, they felt, did not even believe in economic freedom and independence as principles. The airtime that the budding movement received on Fox News had a galvanizing effect, inspiring many citizens who were 'mad as hell' and 'wanted their country back' to become involved (Skocpol and Williamson 2012: 8). The Tea Party's central aim was to restore an earlier, less decadent America founded on republican values, where the undeserving are not pampered with bailouts financed by taxes on hard-working citizens. It identified debt, the unearned, fictitious money used to finance handouts and bailouts, as one of the main factors responsible for the corruption of the American republic, and it demanded austerity as a means to reverse the process of moral decline. In other words, in this case, the resistance to the effects of neoliberalism took the form of a pro-neoliberal populism.

OWS and the Tea Party are dramatically divergent political movements with their origins in very similar sources of instability, and even in very similar political sentiments – both are deeply concerned with the extent to which Washington politics is controlled by corporate and financial elites, and the way this facilitates the kinds of practices that led to the financial crisis. Similar trends have been visible more recently, in the way Bernie Sanders and especially Donald Trump have upset the Democratic and Republican establishments. The electoral success of Sanders was testimony to the extent to which OWS sentiments had spread and come to influence sizeable sections of the Democratic Party. To a significant extent his campaign was energized by the many Democratic voters who had come to see the Clinton administration of the 1990s as an important phase in the reformulation, extension and deepening of neoliberalism, and who viewed Hillary Clinton as embodying continuity with this legacy (Rehmann 2016).

Donald Trump's extraordinary rise to power, meanwhile, embodies some of the most paradoxical characteristics of neoliberalism in an even more flagrant way than the Tea Party did a few years earlier. His support is drawn heavily from the white working and middle classes who see themselves as the backbone of the American nation but feel that their ability to lead a secure economic existence is threatened time and again by a wide variety of external forces (e.g., foreign powers, immigrants, elites, welfare recipients). Trump's candidacy drew tremendous strength from the social injuries that several decades of neoliberal restructuring have produced, even though his life and career exemplify above all privilege and elitism. The figure who has built a movement around such concerns is himself one of the most iconic manifestations of contemporary inequality. Trump's apparent lack of respect for Wall Street finance, his opposition to free trade, his willingness to ally himself with overtly exclusionary political currents, and his admiration for authoritarian leaders are all elements that are not easily integrated into neoliberal business-as-usual. But here we should once again remind ourselves that neoliberalism as a mode of governance

has always played fast-and-loose with such political commitments. Moreover, alongside his promises to tear up NAFTA
and impose sizeable tariffs on Chinese imports, some of his
policies are standard neoliberal fare, such as cutting the rate
of corporate tax from 35 per cent to 15 per cent. At the time
of writing it is not yet clear which, if any, of his professed
commitments will become policy, particularly when considered in the context of a Republican-controlled Congress with
substantial pre-commitments to ongoing neoliberalization.

The relationship between capitalism and democracy has
been no less complex in Europe. On the one hand, organized resistance against the austerity agenda has been highly
significant. Especially in Mediterranean countries, left-wing
political parties and movements have challenged the austerity drive. Syriza in Greece has no doubt received the most
press coverage: it came to power on the strength of a programme that sought to block the EU's plans to enforce debt
repayment by enforcing severe budgetary austerity. As discussed earlier, however, once in power, the Syriza government
had considerable difficulty sticking to its hard-line stance
on the matter, as walking away from the negotiating table
and simply defaulting on the debts involved a degree of risk
for the Greek economy that the government was ultimately
not willing to take (Sheehan 2017). On the other hand, we
should be alert to the fact that the EU's turn to austerity has
met with a considerable degree of public support, evidenced
in the electoral success that conservative parties have enjoyed
in recent years. Although immediately after the crisis anger
at the financial sector was intense and widespread even in
the richer countries of the EU, the ease with which this has
been transformed into a broad-based consensus that 'debts
need to be paid' and that 'there is no such thing as a free
lunch' is remarkable. As a result, the hope has largely disappeared that German and Greek citizens might find solidarity
in recognizing that their problems have common origins in
neoliberal policies. Whereas the state's generosity towards
the bankers had been a source of widespread concern, in the
current conjuncture the anxiety in Western polities is about
excess generosity towards poor countries and immigrants.

Such tensions were manifest in the 2016 UK vote on the
question of whether or not to stay in the European Union.

The relationship between Britain and the EU has of course a long and complex history, and the divisions among elites themselves were a major reason that the issue could become the subject of a referendum in the first place. Many commentators did not consider it possible that Brits would vote to leave the EU, and it was only fairly close to the referendum itself that a 'leave' vote came to be seen as a real possibility. Elites of various ideological stripes did not neglect to point out the disastrous consequences that leaving the EU would entail. And yet this could not stop the tide of anti-EU sentiment. Many leave voters had never perceived that being part of the EU was in any way beneficial to their own lives, and years of political rhetoric about immigration problems and European bureaucracy had struck much more of a chord. That, at any rate, was what motivated a significant proportion of the leave voters, but by all accounts large parts of the electorate were above all minded to cast a protest vote, rejecting the plans of political elites who had let them down for so many years. After all, it was not necessarily clear which option, to leave or to stay, made the most strategic sense, which served to greatly heighten the symbolism of the vote. In so far as the leave vote was a protest vote driven by the discontent with neoliberal policies, it did not provide any guarantees for the future in this regard. Former Chancellor Nigel Lawson (2016) was quick to argue that the break with Europe gave Britain 'a chance to finish the Thatcher revolution'.

Whether that will turn out to be an accurate claim is anyone's guess. But it should certainly serve as a reminder that neoliberalism has often thrived on confusion and political disarray, and that we would be naive to think that its future requires an active embrace of its formal ideological tenets. If this book has at several points cautioned against the tendency among the critics of neoliberalism to assess its viability against rationalist criteria of legitimacy, it has done so not out of a concern to induce a pessimistic outlook, but rather because the recurrent tendency to underestimate the sources of resilience that neoliberalism can access, and to issue premature declarations of its demise, has itself become an obstacle to level-headed assessments and effective political action. The willingness of progressive critics to believe that the financial crisis had put an end to neoliberalism and would usher in a new Keynesian era only stands as the most dramatic and unfortunate example of that problem. The future of neoliberalism is open-ended – not just in the sense that we do not have the right methods or enough data to foresee how it will evolve, but in the sense that it has yet to be made. Those who have an interest in unmaking neo-liberalism have much to gain from a clear perspective on its sources of durability and weakness, and on its recurrent and emerging contradictions.

References

Abramowitz, Mimi. 2006. 'Welfare Reform in the United States: Gender, Race and Class Matter', *Critical Social Policy* 26 (2): 336–64.

Achar, Gilbert. 2013. *The People Want: A Radical Exploration of the Arab Uprising.* Berkeley: University of California Press.

Adkins, Lisa. 2012. 'Out of Work or Out of Time? Rethinking Labor After the Financial Crisis', *South Atlantic Quarterly* 111 (4): 621–41.

Albo, Greg. 1996. 'The World Economy, Market Imperatives and Alternatives', *Monthly Review* 48 (7): 6–22.

Allon, Fiona. 2010. 'Speculating on Everyday Life: The Cultural Economy of the Quotidian', *Journal of Communication Inquiry* 34 (4): 366–81.

Aslund, Anders. 2013. *How Capitalism Was Built: The Transformation of Central and Eastern Europe, Russia, the Caucasus, and Central Asia.* Cambridge: Cambridge University Press.

Ayers, Alison J. and Alfredo Saad-Filho. 2015. 'Democracy Against Neoliberalism: Paradoxes, Limitations, Transcendence', *Critical Sociology* 41 (4–5): 597–618.

Bair, Sheila. 2013. *Bull by the Horns: Fighting to Save Main Street from Wall Street and Wall Street from Itself.* New York: Simon and Schuster.

Baker, Andrew. 2010. 'Restraining Regulatory Capture? Anglo-America, Crisis Politics and Trajectories of Change in Global Financial Governance', *International Affairs* 86 (3): 647–63.

Bakker, Isabella. 2003. 'Neo-Liberal Governance and the Reprivatization of Social Reproduction: Social Provisioning and Shifting Gender Orders', in Isabella Bakker and Stephen Gill (eds), *Power,*

Production and Social Reproduction. London: Palgrave Macmillan, 66–82.

Bambra, Clare, Kayleigh Garthwaite, Alison Copeland and Ben Barr. 2016. 'All In It Together? Health Inequalities, Austerity, and the "Great Recession"', in Kayleigh Smith, Clare Bambra and Sarah E. Hill (eds), *Health Inequalities: Critical Perspectives*. Oxford: Oxford University Press, 164–76.

Barkan, Joshua. 2013. *Corporate Sovereignty: Law and Government Under Capitalism*. Minneapolis: University of Minnesota Press.

Barro, Robert J. and Jong-Wha Lee. 2002. 'IMF Programs: Who is Chosen and What Are the Effects?', *National Bureau of Economic Research Working Paper 8951*, http://www.nber.org/papers/w8951.

Becker, Gary. 1964. *Human Capital Theory*. New York: National Bureau of Economic Research.

Becker, Gary. 1990. *The Economic Approach to Human Behaviour*. Chicago: University of Chicago Press.

Beder, Sharon. 2000. *Global Spin: The Corporate Assault on Environmentalism*. Brunswick: Scribe.

Bendix, Reinhard. 1977. *Nation-Building and Citizenship: Studies of Our Changing Social Order*. Berkeley: University of California Press.

Bengtsson, Erik and Magnus Ryner. 2015. 'The (International) Political Economy of Falling Wage Shares: Situating Working-Class Agency', *New Political Economy* 20 (3): 406–30.

Berry, Albert and John Serieux. 2006. 'Riding the Elephants: The Evolution of World Economic Growth and Income Distribution at the End of the Twentieth Century (1980–2000)', *DESA Working Paper No. 27*.

Birch, Kean. 2015. *We Have Never Been Neoliberal: A Manifesto for a Doomed Youth*. Winchester: Zero Books.

BIS (Bank for International Settlements). 2016. 'Triennial Central Bank Survey Foreign Exchange Turnover in April 2016', http://www.bis.org/publ/rpfx16fx.pdf.

Biven, W. Carl. 2014. *Jimmy Carter's Economy: Policy in an Age of Limits*. Chapel Hill: University of North Carolina Press.

Block, Fred. 2012. 'Varieties of What? Should We Still Be Using the Concept of Capitalism?', *Political Power and Social Theory* 23: 269–91.

Block, Fred and Margaret R. Somers. 2014. *The Power of Market Fundamentalism: Karl Polanyi's Critique*. Cambridge, MA: Harvard University Press.

Blyth, Mark. 2002. *Great Transformations: Economic Ideas and Institutional Change in the Twentieth Century*. Cambridge: Cambridge University Press.

Board of Governors of the Federal Reserve System. 2017. 'Consumer Credit G-19', https://www.federalreserve.gov/releases/g19/HIST/cc_hist_sa_levels.html.

Boas, Taylor C. and Jordan Gans-Morse. 2009. 'Neoliberalism: From New Liberal Philosophy to Anti-Liberal Slogan', *Studies in Comparative International Development* 44 (2): 137–61.

Bolick, Clint. 1995. 'Thatcher's Revolution: Deregulation and Political Transformation', *Yale Journal on Regulation* 12 (2): 527–48.

Bond, Patrick. 2014. *Elite Transition: From Apartheid to Neoliberalism in South Africa*. London: Pluto Press.

Bonefeld, Werner. 2016. 'Authoritarian Liberalism: From Schmitt via Ordoliberalism to the Euro', *Critical Sociology* (7 August, online).

Bourguignon, François and Christian Morrisson. 2002. 'Inequality among World Citizens: 1820–1992', *American Economic Review* 92 (4): 727–44.

Boushey, Heather. 2002. 'The Effects of the Personal Responsibility and Work Opportunity Reconciliation Act on Working Families', *Economic Policy Institute Viewpoints*, http://www.epi.org/publication/webfeatures_viewpoints_tanf_testimony.

Boyer, Robert and Daniel Drache (eds). 1996. *States Against Markets: The Limits of Globalization*. New York: Routledge.

Bradshaw, York W. and Jie Huang. 1991. 'Intensifying Global Dependency: Foreign Debt, Structural Adjustment, and Third World Underdevelopment', *Sociological Quarterly* 32 (3): 321–42.

Braithwaite, John. 2008. *Regulatory Capitalism: How It Works, Ideas for Making It Work Better*. Cheltenham: Edward Elgar.

Brennan, Deborah. 2014. 'The Business of Care: Australia's Experiment with the Marketisation of Childcare', in Lionel Orchard and Chris Miller (eds), *Australian Public Policy: Progressive Ideas in the Neoliberal Ascendency*. Bristol: Policy Press, 151–68.

Brennan, Deborah, Bettina Cass, Susan Himmelweit and Marta Szebehely. 2012. 'The Marketisation of Care: Rationales and Consequences in Nordic and Liberal Care Regimes', *Journal of European Social Policy* 22 (4): 377–91.

Brenner, Neil, Jamie Peck and Nik Theodore. 2010. 'Variegated Neoliberalization: Geographies, Modalities, Pathways', *Global Networks* 10 (2): 182–222.

Brenner, Neil and Nik Theodore. 2002. 'Cities and the Geographies of "Actually Existing Neoliberalism"', *Antipode* 34 (3): 349–79.

Brenner, Robert. 2006. *The Economics of Global Turbulence: The Advanced Capitalist Economies from Long Boom to Long Downturn, 1945–2005*. London: Verso.

Brown, Wendy. 2015. *Undoing the Demos: Neoliberalism's Stealth Revolution*. New York: Zone Books.

Bruff, Ian. 2014. 'The Rise of Authoritarian Neoliberalism', *Rethinking Marxism* 26 (1): 113–29.

Bryan, Dick and Michael Rafferty. 2006. *Capitalism with Derivatives: A Political Economy of Financial Derivatives, Capital and Class.* New York: Palgrave.

Bryan, Dick and Michael Rafferty. 2013. 'Fundamental Value: A Category in Transformation', *Economy & Society* 42 (1): 130–53.

Buchanan, James M., Charles K. Rowley, Albert Breton, Jack Wiseman, Bruno Frey, A. T. Peacock, Jo Grimond, W. A. Niskanen and Martin Ricketts. 1978. *The Economics of Politics.* London: Institute of Economic Affairs.

Buckman, Greg. 2004. *Globalization: Tame It or Scrap It? Mapping the Alternatives of the Anti-Globalization Movement.* London: Zed Books.

Bulow, Jeremy and Kenneth Rogoff. 1990. 'Cleaning up Third World Debt Without Getting Taken to the Cleaners', *Journal of Economic Perspectives* 4 (1): 31–42.

Burgin, Angus. 2012. *The Great Persuasion: Reinventing Free Markets Since the Depression.* Cambridge, MA: Harvard University Press.

Burk, Kathleen and Alec Cairncross. 1992. *Good-Bye, Great Britain: The 1976 IMF Crisis.* New Haven: Yale University Press.

Burton, Michael. 2016. *The Politics of Austerity: A Recent History.* Abingdon: Palgrave.

Bush, Sasha B. 2016. 'Risk Markets and the Landscape of Social Change: Notes on Derivatives, Insurance, and Global Neoliberalism', *International Journal of Political Economy* 45 (2): 124–46.

Cahill, Damien. 2001. 'Why the Right Uses "Class" against the Left', *Arena Journal* 16: 151–62.

Cahill, Damien. 2014. *The End of Laissez-Faire? On the Durability of Embedded Neoliberalism.* Cheltenham: Edward Elgar.

Callinicos, Alex. 2001. *Against the Third Way.* Cambridge: Polity.

Cardoso, Fernando H. and Enzo Faletto. 1979. *Dependency and Development in Latin America.* Berkeley: University of California Press.

Castles, Stephen. 2015. 'Migration, Precarious Work, and Rights', in Ronaldo Munck, Carl-Ulrick Schierup, Branka Likic-Brboric and Anders Neergaard (eds), *Migration, Precarity, and Global Governance: Challenges and Opportunities for Labour.* Oxford: Oxford University Press, 46–67.

CBO (Congressional Budget Office). 2011. 'The Distribution of Household Income and Federal Taxes, 2011', https://www.cbo.gov/publication/49440.

Chorev, Nitsan and Sarah L. Babb. 2009. 'The Crisis of Neoliberalism and the Future of International Institutions: A

Comparison of the IMF and the WTO', *Theory and Society* 38 (5): 459–84.

Clarke, Simon. 1988. *Keynesianism, Monetarism and the Crisis of the State*. Cheltenham: Edward Elgar.

Coates, David. 1980. *Labour in Power? A Study of the Labour Government 1974–79*. London: Longman.

Coates, David. 2000. *Models of Capitalism: Growth and Stagnation in the Modern Era*. Cambridge: Polity.

Cockett, Richard. 1994. *Thinking the Unthinkable: Think Tanks and the Economic Counter-Revolution 1931–1983*. London: HarperCollins.

Collins, Jane L. and Victoria Mayer. 2010. *Both Hands Tied: Welfare Reform and the Race to the Bottom in the Low-Wage Labor Market*. Chicago: University of Chicago Press.

Connolly, William E. 2013. *The Fragility of Things: Self-Organizing Processes, Neoliberal Fantasies, and Democratic Activism*. Durham, NC: Duke University Press.

Cooper, Melinda. 2017. *Family Values: Between Neoliberalism and the New Social Conservatism*. New York: Zone Books.

Cross, Jamie. 2010. 'Neoliberalism as Unexceptional: Economic Zones and the Everyday Precariousness of Working Life in South India', *Critique of Anthropology* 30 (4): 355–73.

Crouch, Colin. 1977. *Class Conflict and the Industrial Relations Crisis: Compromise and Corporatism in the Policies of the British State*. Atlantic Highlands, NJ: Humanities Press.

Crouch, Colin. 2011. *The Strange Non-Death of Neo-Liberalism*. Cambridge: Polity.

Dardot, Pierre and Christian Laval. 2013. *The New Way of the World: On Neoliberal Society*. London: Verso.

Davidson, Neil. 2010. 'What Was Neoliberalism?', in Patricia McCafferty, Neil Davidson and David Miller (eds), *Neoliberal Scotland: Class and Society in a Stateless Nation*. Newcastle upon Tyne: Cambridge Scholars Publishing, 1–89.

Davies, William. 2014. *The Limits of Neoliberalism: Authority, Sovereignty and the Logic of Competition*. London: Sage.

Davis, Gerald. 2009. *Managed by the Markets: How Finance Re-Shaped America*. Oxford: Oxford University Press.

Davis, Mike. 2006. *Planet of Slums*. London: Verso.

De Goede, Marieke. 2001. 'Discourses of Scientific Finance and the Failure of Long-Term Capital Management', *New Political Economy* 6 (2): 149–70.

De Muth, Christopher. 2007. 'Think Tank Confidential', *Wall Street Journal*, 11 October, http://www.wsj.com/articles/SB119206742349355601.

Di Muzio, Tim. 2015. 'The Plutonomy of the 1%: Dominant Ownership and Conspicuous Consumption in the New Gilded Age', *Millennium: Journal of International Studies* 43 (2): 492–510.

Dodwell, Aisha. 2016. 'Corporations Running the World Used to Be Science Fiction – Now It's a Reality', *Global Justice Now*, http://www.globaljustice.org.uk/blog/2016/sep/12/corporations-running-world-used-be-science-fiction-now-its-reality.

Doogan, Kevin. 2009. *New Capitalism? The Transformation of Work*. Cambridge: Polity.

Duménil, Gérard and Dominique Lévy. 2004. *Capital Resurgent: Roots of the Neoliberal Revolution*. Cambridge, MA: Harvard University Press.

Dunn, Bill. 2009. *Global Political Economy: A Marxist Critique*. London: Pluto Press.

Eagleton-Pierce, Matthew. 2016. *Neoliberalism: The Key Concepts*. New York: Routledge.

Ebenstein, Alan. 2001. *Friedrich Hayek: A Biography*. Abingdon: Macmillan.

Ebenstein, Lanny. 2015. *Chicagonomics: The Evolution of Chicago Free Market Economics*. New York: St. Martin's.

Economist. 2013. 'Freedom Fighter', *The Economist*, 13 April.

Ehrenreich, Barbara. 1990. *Fear of Falling: The Inner Life of the Middle Class*. New York: Harper Perennial.

Eichengreen, Barry. 2008. *Globalizing Capital: A History of the International Monetary System*. Second edition. Princeton: Princeton University Press.

Engels, Friedrich. 2009 [1845]. *The Condition of the Working Class in England*. Oxford: Oxford University Press.

Erturk, Ismail, Julie Froud, Sukhdev Johal, Adam Leaver and Karel Williams. 2007. 'The Democratization of Finance? Promises, Outcomes and Conditions', *Review of International Political Economy* 14 (4): 553–75.

Farrant, Andrew and Edward McPhail. 2014. 'Can a Dictator Turn a Constitution into a Can-opener? F. A. Hayek and the Alchemy of Transitional Dictatorship in Chile', *Review of Political Economy* 26 (3): 331–48.

Federal Reserve Bank of St. Louis. 2017. 'U.S. Bureau of Economic Analysis, Real Gross Domestic Product [GDPC1]', https://fred.stlouisfed.org/series/GDPC1.

Felder, Ruth. 2008. 'From Bretton Woods to Neoliberal Reforms: The International Financial Institutions and American Power', in Leo Panitch and Martijn Konings (eds), *American Empire and the Political Economy of Global Finance*. New York: Palgrave, 175–97.

Ferguson, Susan and David McNally. 2015. 'Precarious Migrants: Gender, Race and the Social Reproduction of a Global Working Class', in Leo Panitch and Greg Albo (eds), *The Socialist Register 2015: Transforming Classes*. London: Merlin Press, 1–23.

Feulner, Ed. 1985. 'Ideas, Think-Tanks and Governments: Away from the Power Elite, Back to the People', *Quadrant* (November): 22–6.

Fiszbein, Ariel, Norbert Schady, Francisco Ferreira, Margaret Grosh, Niall Keleher, Pedro Olinto and Emmanuel Skoufias. 2009. *Conditional Cash Transfers: Reducing Present and Future Poverty*. World Bank Policy Research Report. Washington, DC: World Bank, https://openknowledge.worldbank.org/handle/10986/2597.

Foucault, Michel. 2008 [1979]. *The Birth of Biopolitics*. New York: Palgrave.

Fourcade-Gourinchas, Marion and Sarah L. Babb. 2002. 'The Rebirth of the Liberal Creed: Paths to Neoliberalism in Four Countries', *American Journal of Sociology* 108 (3): 533–79.

Frank, Andre Gunder. 1978. *Dependent Accumulation and Under-Development*. London: Macmillan.

Frank, Thomas. 2005. *What's the Matter with Kansas? How Conservatives Won the Heart of America*. New York: Holt.

Fraser, Nancy. 2014. 'Can Society Be Commodities All the Way Down? Post-Polanyian Reflections on Capitalist Crisis', *Economy and Society* 43 (4): 541–58.

Fredriksen, Kaja. 2012. 'Income Inequality in the European Union', OECD Economics Department Working Papers 952, http://www.oecd.org/officialdocuments/publicdisplaydocumentpdf/?cote=ECO/WKP(2012)29&docLanguage=En.

Friedman, Milton. 2002. *Capitalism and Freedom*. Chicago: University of Chicago Press.

Friedman, Milton. 2012. 'Neo-Liberalism and Its Prospects', in Lanny Ebenstein (ed.), *The Indispensable Milton Friedman: Essays on Politics and Economics*. Washington, DC: Regnery Publishing, 3–9.

Friedman, Milton and Rose Friedman. 1980. *Free to Choose: A Personal Statement*. Harmondsworth: Penguin.

Friedman, Milton and Rose Friedman. 2002. 'Interview with Milton and Rose Friedman by Michael Mcfaul', http://newmedia.ufm.edu/gsm/index.php?title=Interview_with_Rose_and_Milton_Friedman.

Froud, Julie, Sukhdev Johal, Adam Leaver and Karel Williams. 2006. *Financialization and Strategy: Narrative and Numbers*. Abingdon: Routledge.

Fuchs, Doris. 2007. *Business Power in Global Governance*. London: Lynne Rienner.

Fukuyama, Francis. 1992. *The End of History and the Last Man*. New York: Free Press.

Fuller, Gregory W. 2016. *The Great Debt Transformation: Households, Financialization, and Policy Responses*. New York: Palgrave.

Gamble, Andrew. 1988. *The Free Economy and the Strong State: The Politics of Thatcherism*. Durham, NC: Duke University Press.

Gane, Nicholas. 2014. 'The Emergence of Neoliberalism: Thinking Through and Beyond Michel Foucault's Lectures on Biopolitics', *Theory, Culture & Society* 31 (4): 3–27.

George, Susan. 2015. *Shadow Sovereigns: How Global Corporations Are Seizing Power*. Cambridge: Polity.

Ghizoni, Sanra. 2013. 'Nixon Ends Convertibility of US Dollars into Gold and Announces Wage/Price Controls', Federal Reserve History, http://www.federalreservehistory.org/Events/DetailView/33.

Gill, Stephen. 2016. 'Transnational Class Formations, European Crisis and the Silent Revolution', *Critical Sociology* (4 August, online).

Gills, Barry K. 2008. 'The Swinging of the Pendulum: The Global Crisis and Beyond', *Globalizations* 5 (4): 513–22.

Gingrich, Jane. 2011. *Making Markets in the Welfare State: The Politics of Varying Market Reforms*. Cambridge: Cambridge University Press.

Gledhill, Malcolm. 2016. 'Serco Group Plc'. Hoover's Company Records.

Glyn, Andrew. 2006. *Capitalism Unleashed: Finance, Globalization and Welfare*. Oxford: Oxford University Press.

Gowan, Peter. 1999. *The Global Gamble: Washington's Faustian Bid for World Dominance*. London: Verso.

Grahl, John and Photis Lysandrou. 2006. 'Capital Market Trading Volume: An Overview and Some Preliminary Conclusions', *Cambridge Journal of Economics* 30 (6): 955–79.

Greider, William. 1987. *Secrets of the Temple: How the Federal Reserve Runs the Country*. New York: Simon and Schuster.

Greig, Alastair, David Hulme and Mark Turner. 2007. *Challenging Global Inequality: Development Theory and Practice in the 21st Century*. New York: Palgrave.

Guardian. 2013. 'UK Total Public Spending Since 1963', 18 March.

Habermas, Jürgen. 1975. *Legitimation Crisis*. New York: Beacon Press.

Hacker, Jacob and Paul Pierson. 2010. 'Winner-Take-All Politics: Public Policy, Political Organization, and the Precipitous Rise of Top Incomes in the United States', *Politics and Society* 38 (2): 152–204.

Hackworth, Jason. 2007. *The Neoliberal City*. Ithaca: Cornell University Press.

Hackworth, Jason. 2012. *Faith Based: Religious Neoliberalism and the Politics of Welfare in the United States*. Athens: University of Georgia Press.

Hall, Stuart. 1979. 'The Great Moving Right Show', *Marxism Today* (January): 14–20.

Hamm, Patrick, Lawrence King and David Stuckler. 2012. 'Mass Privatization, State Capacity, and Economic Growth in Post-Communist Countries', *American Sociological Review* 77 (2): 295–324.

Harmon, Mark D. 1997. *The British Labour Government and the 1976 IMF Crisis*. New York: St. Martin's.

Harris, John. 2013. 'Serco: The Company That is Running Britain', *Guardian*, https://www.theguardian.com/business/2013/jul/29/serco-biggest-company-never-heard-of.

Harvey, David. 2005. *A Brief History of Neoliberalism*. Oxford: Oxford University Press.

Hatcher, Daniel L. 2016. *The Poverty Industry: The Exploitation of America's Most Vulnerable Citizens*. New York: New York University Press.

Hay, Colin. 1996. *Re-Stating Social and Political Change*. Buckingham: Open University Press.

Hayek, Friedrich. 1945. *The Road to Serfdom*. Chicago: University of Chicago Press.

Hayek, Friedrich. 1949. *Individualism and Economic Order*. London: Routledge & Kegan Paul.

Hayek, Friedrich. 1973. *Law, Legislation and Liberty: A New Statement of the Liberal Principles of Justice and Political Economy*, Vol. 1, *Rules and Order*. Chicago: University of Chicago Press.

Hayek, Friedrich. 1976a. *Denationalisation of Money*. London: Institute of Economic Affairs.

Hayek, Friedrich. 1976b. *Law, Legislation and Liberty: A New Statement of the Liberal Principles of Justice and Political Economy*, Vol. 2, *The Mirage of Social Justice*. London: Routledge & Kegan Paul.

Hayek, Friedrich. 1988. *The Fatal Conceit: The Errors of Socialism*. London: Routledge.

Hayek, Friedrich. 2006. *The Constitution of Liberty*. London: Routledge.

Heatherly, Charles (ed.). 1981. *Mandate for Leadership: Policy Management in a Conservative Administration*. Washington, DC: Heritage Foundation.

Helleiner, Eric. 1994. *States and the Reemergence of Global Finance: From Bretton Woods to the 1990s*. Ithaca: Cornell University Press.

Herod, Andrew and Rob Lambert. 2016. 'Neoliberalism, Precarious Work and Remaking the Geography of Global Capitalism', in Rob Lambert and Andrew Herod (eds), *Neoliberal Capitalism and Precarious Work: Ethnographies of Accommodation and Resistance*. Northampton: Edward Elgar, 1–42.

Heyes, Jason. 2013. 'Flexicurity in Crisis: European Labour Market Policies in a Time of Austerity', *European Journal of Industrial Relations* 19 (1): 71–86.

Heyes, Jason, Paul Lewis and Ian Clark. 2012. 'Varieties of Capitalism, Neoliberalism and the Economic Crisis of 2008–?', *Industrial Relations Journal* 43 (3): 222–41.

Hjelmgaard, Kim. 2013. 'Thatcher Was Master of the Free Market', *USA Today*, http://www.usatoday.com/story/news/world/2013/04/08/thatcher-economic-impact/2063591.

Hobsbawm, Eric. 1989. *The Age of Empire: 1875–1914*. New York: Vintage.

Hobsbawm, Eric. 1996. *The Age of Extremes: A History of the World, 1914–1991*. New York: Vintage.

Hogan, Michael J. 1987. *The Marshall Plan: America, Britain and the Reconstruction of Western Europe, 1947–1952*. Cambridge: Cambridge University Press.

Hourani, Najib. 2014. 'Neoliberal Urbanism and the Arab Uprising: A View From Amman', *Journal of Urban Affairs* 36 (2): 650–62.

Howarth, David J. 2001. *The French Road to the European Monetary Union*. New York: Palgrave.

Hudson, Michael. 2005. *Global Fracture: The New International Economic Order*. London: Pluto Press.

Hudson, Michael. 2014. *The Bubble and Beyond*. New York: ISLET.

Humphrys, Elizabeth and Damien Cahill. 2016. 'How Labour Made Neoliberalism', *Critical Sociology* (4 August, online).

Idso, Craig, Robert Carter and Fred Singer. 2015. 'Why Scientists Disagree About Global Warming', *The Heartland Institute*, https://www.heartland.org/publications-resources/publications/why-scientists-disagree-about-global-warming.

ILO. 2015. 'World Employment and Social Outlook 2015: The Changing Nature of Jobs', http://www.ilo.org/global/research/global-reports/weso/2015-changing-nature-of-jobs/lang–en/index.htm.

IMF. 2004. 'IMF Concessional Financing Through Esaf – Fact Sheet 2004', http://www.imf.org/external/np/exr/facts/esaf.htm.

ITUC. 2011. *Living with Economic Insecurity: Women in Precarious Work*. International Trade Union Confederation.

Jessop, Bob. 2002. 'Liberalism, Neoliberalism, and Urban Governance: A State–Theoretical Perspective', *Antipode* 34 (3): 452–72.

Jessop, Bob. 2003. 'From Thatcherism to New Labour: Neo-liberalism, Workfarism, and Labour Market Regulation', http://www.lancaster.ac.uk/fass/resources/sociology-online-papers/papers/jessop-from-thatcherism-to-new-labour.pdf.

Joyce, Joseph P. 2012. *The IMF and Global Financial Crises: Phoenix Rising?* Oxford: Oxford University Press.

Judis, John. 2016. *Populist Explosion: How the Great Recession Transformed American and European Politics*. Columbia Global Reports.

Kiely, Ray. 2007. *The New Political Economy of Development: Globalization, Imperialism, Hegemony*. Abingdon: Palgrave Macmillan.

Kiersey, Nicholas J. 2011. 'Everyday Neoliberalism and the Subjectivity of Crisis: Post-Political Control in an Era of Financial Turmoil', *Journal of Critical Globalisation Studies* 4: 23–44.

Kindleberger, Charles. 1989. *The World in Depression, 1929–1939*. Berkeley: University of California Press.

Klein, Naomi. 2001. 'Reclaiming the Commons', *New Left Review* 9 (May–June): 81–9.

Klein, Naomi. 2008. *The Shock Doctrine: The Rise of Disaster Capitalism*. New York: Picador.

Koeber, Charles. 2011. 'Consumptive Labor: The Increasing Importance of Consumers in the Labor Process', *Humanity and Society* 35 (3): 205–32.

Konings, Martijn. 2010. 'Renewing State Theory', *Politics* 30 (3): 174–82.

Konings, Martijn. 2011. *The Development of American Finance*. Cambridge: Cambridge University Press.

Konings, Martijn. 2015. *The Emotional Logic of Capitalism: What Progressives Have Missed*. Stanford: Stanford University Press.

Konings, Martijn. 2018. *Capital and Time: For a New Critique of Neoliberal Reason*. Stanford: Stanford University Press.

Kozol, Jonathan. 2006. *The Shame of the Nation: The Restoration of Apartheid Schooling in America*. New York: Broadway Books.

Kozol, Jonathan. 2012. *Savage Inequalities: Children in America's Schools*. New York: Broadway Books.

Krippner, Greta R. 2005. 'The Financialization of the American Economy', *Socio-Economic Review* 3 (2): 173–208.

Krugman, Paul. 2009. *The Conscience of a Liberal*. New York: W. W. Norton and Company.

Langley, Paul. 2008. *The Everyday Life of Global Finance: Saving and Borrowing in Anglo-America*. Oxford: Oxford University Press.

Lawrence, Robert Z. and Lawrence Edwards. 2013. 'US Employment Deindustrialization: Insights from History and the International

Experience', *Peterson Institute for International Economics*. Policy Brief PB13–27.

Lawson, Nigel. 2016. 'Brexit Gives Us a Chance to Finish the Thatcher Revolution', *Financial Times*, 2 September.

Lee, Benjamin and Randy Martin (eds). 2016. *Derivatives and the Wealth of Societies*. Chicago: University of Chicago Press.

Leicht, Kevin T., Tony Walter, Ivan Sainsaulieu and Scott Davies. 2009. 'New Public Management and New Professionalism across Nations and Contexts', *Current Sociology* 57 (4): 581–605.

Leyshon, Andrew and Nigel Thrift. 2007. 'The Capitalization of Almost Everything: The Future of Finance and Capitalism', *Theory, Culture & Society* 24 (7–8): 97–115.

Lippman, Walter. 1937. *The Good Society*. Boston: Little, Brown and Company.

LiPuma, Edward and Benjamin Lee. 2004. *Financial Derivatives and the Globalization of Risk*. Durham, NC: Duke University Press.

Lowenstein, Roger. 2001. *When Genius Failed: The Rise and Fall of Long-Term Capital Management*. New York: Random House.

Lowenstein, Roger. 2004. *Origins of the Crash: The Great Bubble and Its Undoing*. New York: Penguin Books.

Lucas, Robert. 1976. 'Econometric Policy Evaluation: A Critique', *Carnegie-Rochester Conference Series* 1: 19–46.

Luna, Juan P. and Fernando Filgueira. 2009. 'The Left Turns as Multiple Paradigmatic Crises', *Third World Quarterly* 30 (2): 371–95.

McCarty, Nolan. 2013. 'Complexity, Capacity, and Capture', in Daniel Carpenter and David A. Moss (eds), *Preventing Regulatory Capture: Special Interest Influence and How to Limit It*. Cambridge: Cambridge University Press, 99–123.

McKinsey Global Institute. 2016. 'Poorer Than Their Parents? Flat or Falling Incomes in Advanced Economies', McKinsey and Company.

McLean, Bethany. 2016. 'Payday Lending: Will Anything Better Replace It?' *The Atlantic*, May.

McMichael, Philip. 2012. *Development and Social Change: A Global Perspective*. London: Sage.

McNally, David. 2006. *Another World Is Possible: Globalization and Anti-Capitalism*. Winnipeg: Arbeiter Ring.

Maddison Project. 2013. 'Database', http://www.ggdc.net/maddison/ maddison-project/data.htm.

Mahler, Vincent A., David K. Jesuit and Piotr R. Paradowski. 2013. 'Political Sources of Government Redistribution in High-Income Countries', in Janet C. Gornick and Markus Jantti (eds), *Income*

Inequality: Economic Disparities and the Middle Class in Affluent Countries. Stanford: Stanford University Press, 145–72.

Marston, Greg and Lynda Shevellar. 2014. 'In the Shadow of the Welfare State: The Role of Payday Lending in Poverty Survival in Australia', *Journal of Social Policy* 43 (1): 155–72.

Martin, Randy. 2002. *Financialization of Daily Life*. Philadelphia: Temple University Press.

Mead, Lawrence. 1986. *Beyond Entitlement: The Social Obligations of Citizenship*. New York: Free Press.

Mead, Lawrence. 1993. *The New Politics of Poverty: The Nonworking Poor in America*. New York: Basic Books.

Mikler, John. 2013. 'Global Companies as Actors in Global Policy and Governance', in John Mikler (ed.), *The Handbook of Global Companies*. Chichester: John Wiley, 1–16.

Milanović, Branko. 2009. 'Global Inequality and the Global Inequality Extraction Ratio: The Story of the Past Two Centuries', World Bank Policy Research Working Paper 5044.

Mirowski, Philip. 2013. *Never Let a Serious Crisis Go to Waste: How Neoliberalism Survived the Financial Meltdown*. London: Verso.

Modigliani, Franco. 1988. 'Reagan's Economic Policies: A Critique', *Oxford Economic Papers* 40 (3): 397–426.

Molnar, Michele. 2013. 'Back-to-School Time Brings New Corporate Sponsorship', *Edweek Market Brief*, https://marketbrief.edweek.org/marketplace-k-12/back-to-school_time_brings_new_corporate_sponsorships.

Montgomerie, Johnna. 2009. 'The Pursuit of (Past) Happiness? Middle-Class Indebtedness and American Financialisation', *New Political Economy* 14 (1): 1–24.

Moody, Kim. 1987. 'Reagan, the Business Agenda and the Collapse of Labor', *Socialist Register* 23: 153–76.

Mudge, Stephanie L. 2008. 'What is Neo-Liberalism?', *Socio-Economic Review* 6 (4): 703–31.

Munck, Ronaldo. 2002. *Globalisation and Labour: The New 'Great Transformation'*. London: Zed Books.

Murray, Charles. 1984. *Losing Ground: American Social Policy, 1950–1980*. New York: Basic Books.

Nik-Khah, Edward. 2011. 'Building Chicago Economics: New Perspectives on the History of America's Most Powerful Economics Program', in Robert Van Horn, Philip Mirowski and Tom Stapleford (eds), *Building Chicago Economics: New Perspectives on the History of America's Most Powerful Economics Program*. Cambridge: Cambridge University Press, 116–47.

Odell, John S. 1982. *U.S. International Monetary Policy: Markets, Power and Ideas as Sources of Change*. Princeton: Princeton University Press.

OECD. 2012. *Employment Outlook 2012*. Paris: OECD Publishing.

OECD. 2016a. 'Long Term Unemployment Rate', https://data.oecd. org/unemp/long-term-unemployment-rate.htm.

OECD. 2016b. 'Statistics: Trade Union Density', https://stats.oecd. org/Index.aspx?DataSetCode=UN_DEN.

Offe, Claus. 1984. *Contradictions of the Welfare State*. Cambridge, MA: MIT Press.

Ong, Aihwa. 2006. *Neoliberalism as Exception: Mutations in Citizenship and Sovereignty*. Durham, NC: Duke University Press.

Orhangazi, Ozgur. 2008. *Financialization and the US Economy*. Cheltenham: Edward Elgar.

Ostry, Jonathan D., Prakash Loungani and Davide Furceri. 2016. 'Neoliberalism: Oversold?' *Finance and Development* 53 (2): 38–41.

Oxfam. 2016. *An Economy for the 1%: How Privilege and Power in the Economy Drive Extreme Inequality and How This Can Be Stopped*, Oxfam Briefing Paper 210.

Panitch, Leo. 1976. *Social Democracy and Industrial Militancy: The Labour Party, the Trade Unions and Incomes Policy, 1945–74*. Cambridge: Cambridge University Press.

Panitch, Leo. 1994. 'Globalisation and the State', *Socialist Register* 30: 60–93.

Panitch, Leo. 2000. 'The New Imperial State', *New Left Review* II/2: 5–20.

Panitch, Leo and Sam Gindin. 2012. *The Making of Global Capitalism: The Political Economy of American Empire*. London and New York: Verso.

Peck, Jamie. 2001. *Workfare States*. New York: Guilford Press.

Peck, Jamie. 2010. *Constructions of Neoliberal Reason*. Oxford: Oxford University Press.

Peck, Jamie. 2011. 'Orientation: In Search of the Chicago School', in Robert Van Horn, Philip Mirowski and Thomas Stapleford (eds), *Building Chicago Economics: New Perspectives on the History of America's Most Powerful Economics Program*. Cambridge: Cambridge University Press, xxv–lii.

Peck, Jamie and Adam Tickell. 2002. 'Neoliberalizing Space', *Antipode* 34 (3): 380–404.

Peck, Jamie and Nik Theodore. 2000. ' "Work First": Workfare and the Regulation of Contingent Labour Markets', *Cambridge Journal of Economics* 24 (1): 119–38.

Peck, Jamie and Nik Theodore. 2010. 'Recombinant Workfare, Across the Americas: Transnationalizing "Fast" Social Policy', *Geoforum* 41 (2): 195–208.

Peet, Richard. 2003. *Unholy Trinity: The IMF, World Bank and WTO*. London: Zed Books.

Phillips-Fein, Kim. 2009. 'Business Conservatives and the Mont Pelerin Society', in Philip Mirowski and Dieter Plehwe (eds), *The Road from Mont Pelerin: The Making of the Neoliberal Thought Collective*. Cambridge, MA: Harvard University Press, 280–301.

Piketty, Thomas. 2014. *Capital in the Twenty-First Century*. Cambridge, MA: Harvard University Press.

Piven, Frances F. and Richard Cloward. 1971. *Regulating the Poor: The Functions of Public Welfare*. New York: Vintage.

Piven, Frances F. and Richard Cloward. 1985. *The New Class War: Reagan's Attack on the Welfare State and Its Consequences*. New York: Pantheon Books.

Plehwe, Dieter. 2009. 'Introduction', in Philip Mirowski and Dieter Plehwe (eds), *The Road from Mont Pelerin: The Making of the Neoliberal Thought Collective*. Cambridge, MA: Harvard University Press.

Polanyi, Karl. 1944. *The Great Transformation*. New York: Farrar & Rinehart.

Prasad, Monica. 2006. *The Politics of Free Markets: The Rise of Neoliberal Economic Policies in Britain, France, Germany, and the United States*. Chicago: University of Chicago Press.

Przeworski, Adam. 1992. 'The Neoliberal Fallacy', *Journal of Democracy* 3 (3): 45–59.

Ptak, Ralph. 2009. 'Neoliberalism in Germany: Revisiting the Ordoliberal Foundations of the Social Market Economy', in Philip Mirowski and Dieter Plehwe (eds), *The Road from Mont Pelerin: The Making of the Neoliberal Thought Collective*. Cambridge, MA: Harvard University Press, 98–138.

Reagan, Ronald. 1981. 'Inaugural Address', http://www.presidency.ucsb.edu/ws/?pid=43130.

Rehmann, Jan. 2016. 'Bernie Sanders and the Hegemonic Crisis of Neoliberal Capitalism: What Next?' *Socialism and Democracy* 30 (3): 1–11.

Roach, Brian. 2005. 'A Primer on Multinational Corporations', in Alfred Chandler and Bruce Mazlish (eds), *Leviathans: Multinational Corporations and the New Global History*. Cambridge: Cambridge University Press, 19–44.

Roberts, Adrienne. 2013. 'Financing Social Reproduction: The Gendered Relations of Debt and Mortgage Finance in Twenty-First-Century America', *New Political Economy* 18 (1): 21–42.

Ronit, Karsten and D. Jensen. 2014. 'Obesity and Industry Self-Regulation of Food and Beverage Marketing: A Literature Review', *European Journal of Clinical Nutrition* 68 (7): 753–9.

Rose, Nikolas. 1993. 'Government, Authority and Expertise in Advanced Liberalism', *Economy & Society* 22 (3): 283–99.

Rostow, Walt W. 1960. *The Stages of Economic Growth*. Cambridge: Cambridge University Press.

Roy, Ananya. 2010. *Poverty Capital*. London: Routledge.

Ruccio, David F. 2011. *Development and Globalization: A Marxian Class Analysis*. London and New York: Routledge.

Ruggie, John. 1982. 'International Regimes, Transactions, and Change: Embedded Liberalism and the Postwar Economic Order', *International Organization* 36 (2): 379–415.

Ryner, Magnus. 2015. 'Europe's Ordoliberal Iron Cage: Critical Political Economy, the Euro Area Crisis and its Management', *Journal of European Public Policy* 22 (2): 275–94.

Saad-Filho, Alfredo. 2007. 'Monetary Policy in the Neoliberal Transition: A Political Economy Review of Keynesianism, Monetarism and Inflation Targeting', in R. Jessop, R. Albritton and R. Westra (eds), *Political Economy and Global Capitalism: The 21st Century, Present and Future*. London: Anthem Press, 89–119.

Sachs, Jeffrey. 1990. 'What Is to Be Done?' *The Economist*, 13 January.

Sachs, Jeffrey D. and Howard J. Shatz. 1994. 'Trade and Jobs in U.S. Manufacturing', *Brookings Papers on Economic Activity* 1: 1–84.

Sanz, Ismael and Francisco Velázquez. 2007. 'The Role of Ageing in the Growth of Government and Social Welfare Spending in the OECD', *European Journal of Political Economy* 23 (4): 917–31.

Sassoon, Donald. 1996. *One Hundred Years of Socialism: The West European Left in the Twentieth Century*. London: I.B. Tauris.

Schram, Sanford F. 2015. *The Return of Ordinary Capitalism: Neoliberalism, Precarity, Occupy*. Oxford: Oxford University Press.

Scruton, Roger. 2006. 'Hayek and Conservatism', in Edward Feser (ed.), *The Cambridge Companion to Hayek*. Cambridge: Cambridge University Press, 208–31.

Seabrooke, Leonard. 2001. *US Power in International Finance: The Victory of Dividends*. Basingstoke: Palgrave.

Serra, Narcís and Joseph E. Stiglitz (eds). 2008. *The Washington Consensus Reconsidered: Towards a New Global Governance*. Oxford: Oxford University Press.

Sheehan, Helene. 2017. *Syriza Wave: Surging and Crashing with the Greek Left*. New York: Monthly Review Press.

Shiller, Robert J. 2004. *The New Financial Order: Risk in the 21st Century*. Princeton: Princeton University Press.

Silber, William L. 2012. *Volcker: The Triumph of Persistence*. New York: Bloomsbury.

Singer, Peter W. 2003. *Corporate Warriors: The Rise of the Privatized Military Industry*. Ithaca: Cornell University Press.

Skocpol, Theda and Vanessa Williamson. 2012. *The Tea Party and the Remaking of Republican Conservatism*. Oxford: Oxford University Press.

Soederberg, Susanne. 2004. *The Politics of the New International Financial Architecture: Reimposing Neoliberal Domination in the Global South*. London: Zed Books.

Soederberg, Susanne. 2005. 'Recasting Neoliberal Dominance in the Global South? A Critique of the Monterrey Consensus', *Alternatives: Global, Local, Political* 30 (3): 325–64.

Soederberg, Susanne. 2014. *Debtfare States and the Poverty Industry: Money, Discipline and the Surplus Population*. Abingdon: Routledge.

Sokol, Martin. 2001. 'Central and Eastern Europe a Decade after the Fall of State-Socialism: Regional Dimensions of Transition Processes', *Regional Studies* 35 (7): 645–55.

Soss, Joe, Richard C. Fording and Sanford Schram. 2011. *Disciplining the Poor: Neoliberal Paternalism and the Persistent Power of Race*. Chicago: University of Chicago Press.

Standing, Guy. 2011. *The Precariat: The New Dangerous Class*. London: Bloomsbury Academic.

Stavrianos, Leften S. 1981. *Global Rift: The Third World Comes of Age*. New York: William Morrow & Co.

Steadman Jones, Daniel. 2012. *Masters of the Universe: Hayek, Friedman, and the Birth of Neoliberal Politics*. Princeton: Princeton University Press.

Stigler, George J. 1971. 'The Economic Theory of Regulation', *Bell Journal of Economics* 2 (1): 3–21.

Stiglitz, Joseph E. 2002. *Globalization and Its Discontents*. New York: Basic Books.

Strange, Susan. 1998. *Mad Money*. Manchester: Manchester University Press.

Streeck, Wolfgang. 2015. 'Heller, Schmitt and the Euro', *European Law Journal* 21 (3): 361–70.

Sugrue, Thomas J. 2014. *The Origins of the Urban Crisis: Race and Inequality in Postwar Detroit*. Princeton: Princeton University Press.

Thatcher, Margaret. 1979. 'Margaret Thatcher Letter to Friedrich Hayek', http://fc95d419f4478b3b6e5f-3f71d0fe2b653c4f00f321 75760e96e7.r87.cf1.rackcdn.com/5F375B2C1D134B84951D72 60F2664CF8.pdf.

Tompson, William. 2009. *The Political Economy of Reform: Lessons from Pensions, Product Markets and Labour Markets in Ten OECD Countries*. Paris: OECD.

Tupy, Marian L. 2015. 'Stop Obsessing About Inequality. It's Actually Decreasing Around the World', *Washington Post*, 8 January.

Van Apeldoorn, Bastiaan. 2009. 'The Contradictions of "Embedded Neoliberalism" and Europe's Multi-Level Legitimacy Crisis: The European Project and its Limits', in Bastiaan van Apeldoorn, Jan Drahokoupil and Laura Horn (eds), *Contradictions and Limits of Neoliberal European Governance: From Lisbon to Lisbon*. New York: Palgrave Macmillan, 21–43.

Van Apeldoorn, Bastiaan. 2014. 'The European Capitalist Class and the Crisis of its Hegemonic Project', *Socialist Register 50*: 189–206.

Van Horn, Rob. 2009. 'Reinventing Monopoly and the Role of Corporations: The Roots of Chicago Law and Economics', in Philip Mirowski and Dieter Plehwe (eds), *The Road from Mont Pelerin: The Making of the Neoliberal Thought Collective*. Cambridge, MA: Harvard University Press, 204–37.

Veltmeyer, Harry, James Petras and Steve Vieux. 1997. 'The Economic Recovery of Latin America: The Myth and the Reality', in Harry Veltmeyer, James Petras and Steve Vieux (eds), *Neoliberalism and Class Conflict in Latin America*. New York: Palgrave, 123–37.

Venugopal, Rajesh. 2015. 'Neoliberalism as Concept', *Economy & Society* 44 (2): 165–87.

Vogel, Steven K. 1998. *Freer Markets, More Rules: Regulatory Reform in Advanced Industrial Countries*. Ithaca: Cornell University Press.

Wacquant, Loic. 2009. *Punishing the Poor: The Neoliberal Government of Social Insecurity*. Durham, NC: Duke University Press.

Wacquant, Loic. 2012. 'Three Steps to a Historical Anthropology of Actually Existing Neoliberalism', *Social Anthropology* 20 (1): 66–79.

Wade, Robert. 2008. 'Financial Regime Change?' *New Left Review* 53: 5–21.

Waisanen, Bert. 2010. *State Tax and Expenditure Limits – 2010*. National Conference of State Legislatures.

Walker, Jeremy and Melinda Cooper. 2011. 'Genealogies of Resilience: From Systems Ecology to the Political Economy of Crisis Adaptation', *Security Dialogue* 42 (2): 143–60.

Walton, John and David Seddon. 1994. *Free Markets and Food Riots: The Politics of Global Adjustment*. Oxford: Blackwell.

White, Michael. 2013. 'Margaret Thatcher Dead at 87 Following Stroke', *Guardian*, 8 April.

Wildau, Gabriel and Tom Mitchell. 2016. 'China Income Inequality Among World's Worst', *Financial Times*, 14 January.

Wilkes, Stephen. 2013. *The Political Power of the Business Corporation*. Cheltenham: Edward Elgar.

Wilkinson, Richard and Kate Pickett. 2011. *The Spirit Level: Why Greater Equality Makes Societies Stronger*. London: Bloomsbury.

Wilson, William Julius. 1997. *When Work Disappears: The World of the New Urban Poor*. New York: Vintage.

Wolfe, Joel. 1991. 'State Power and Ideology in Britain: Mrs Thatcher's Privatization Programme', *Political Studies* 39 (2): 237–52.

Wood, Ellen Meiksins. 1995. *Democracy Against Capitalism: Renewing Historical Materialism*. Cambridge: Cambridge University Press.

Wood, Ellen Meiksins. 2005. *Empire of Capital*. London: Verso.

World Bank. 2016. 'GDP (Current $US)', http://data.worldbank.org/indicator/NY.GDP.MKTP.CD.

Yates, Julian S. and Karen Bakker. 2014. 'Debating the "Post-Neoliberal Turn" in Latin America', *Progress in Human Geography* 38 (1): 62–90.

Index